ZUZU BAILEY'S
It's a Wonderful Life
COOKBOOK

ZUZU BAILEY'S *It's a Wonderful Life* COOKBOOK

Recipes and Anecdotes
Inspired by America's Favorite Movie

KAROLYN GRIMES
AND
FRANKLIN DOHANYOS

CITADEL PRESS
KENSINGTON PUBLISHING CORP.
www.kensingtonbooks.com

CITADEL PRESS books are published by

Kensington Publishing Corp.
850 Third Avenue
New York, NY 10022

All Kensington titles, imprints, and distributed lines are available at special quantity discounts for bulk purchases for sales promotions, premiums, fund raising, educational, or institutional use. Special book excerpts or customized printings can also be created to fit specific needs. For details, write or phone the office of the Kensington special sales manager: Kensington Publishing Corp., 850 Third Avenue, New York, NY 10022, attn: Special Sales Department, phone 1-800-221-2647.

First printing October 2000

10 9 8 7 6 5 4 3 2

Printed in the United States of America

Library of Congress Cataloging-in-Publication Data

Grimes, Karolyn.
Zuzu Bailey's It's a wonderful life cookbook : recipes and anecdotes inspired by America's favorite movie / Karolyn Grimes, Franklin Dohanyos.
p. cm.
"A Citadel Press book."
ISBN 0-8065-2165-1 (pbk.)
1. Cookery. 2. It's a wonderful life (Motion picture) I. Dohanyos, Franklin.
TX714.G76 1996
641.5—dc20 96-31483
CIP

Dedication

This book is dedicated to all the George Baileys in the world who feel that their dreams have not been fulfilled . . . May you realize that you have enriched many lives for the betterment of mankind. And to *the* George Bailey, alias Jimmy Stewart, who reminds us that *no man is a failure who has friends*. Also, a special thank-you to Frank Capra, for reminding us that we can capture and keep the spirit of love for one another alive! —*K.G.*

Writer's Thank-You

To my beautiful wife, Jean, who opened her heart and gave me inspiration, and to Fiona, my own little gingersnap, whose energy and spirit keeps me young at heart, and to my son, Jordan, the newest of our group. —*F.D.*

George Bailey comforts daughter Zuzu before giving her rose a drink.

Contents

Acknowledgments

We offer heartfelt thanks to the following people for all their support in helping to complete this labor of love: Jimmy Stewart, Jimmy Hawkins, Carol Coombs Mueller, Argentina Brunetti, Virginia Patton Moss, Todd Karns, Bobbie Anderson, John Strauss, Grover Asmus, Jean "Beaner" Dohanyos, Bill Krout, Barry Shulman, Collectors Books, and Cinema Collectors.

ZUZU BAILEY'S

It's a Wonderful Life

COOKBOOK

A publicity shot of Karolyn Grimes at age four.

A Note From Zuzu

For the last ten years, Zuzu Bailey from *It's a Wonderful Life* has become my alter ego, as there has been a profound renewed interest in the movie. So many people have a common bond with *It's a Wonderful Life* that I thought you might enjoy reading some of the interesting stories that have surfaced since my days as Zuzu Bailey. I've included my reminiscences below, and over the years I've collected stories from cast and crew members. These are credited and scattered throughout the book.

Making a movie is certainly a strange experience because nothing is real, and scenes are not shot in the sequence viewers see them in. I always thought it was odd that my bedroom was upstairs in *It's a Wonderful Life*, but in reality, those stairs lead to nowhere. There was nothing up there. My bedroom was actually on the main level, but in a different part of the set. That's Hollywood!

I will always remember how gentle and patient Mr. Stewart was throughout the film, especially the scene when he returns from the bridge. He runs upstairs to greet the kids and races back down with me on his back, Tommy under

his arm, and Peter and Janie trying to hug him. For some reason this scene had to be shot several times, which would make anyone cranky. Mr. Stewart never complained and always had a smile on his face.

Have you ever wondered where the name Zuzu came from? Around the turn of the century there was a company called the National Biscuit Company. They made many delicious things, including a product with a happy little clown on the container. It was called Zuzu's Gingersnaps. A friend of mine located one of these cookie tins, and I ended up trading some baseball cards for it!

I travel throughout the country doing Zuzu appearances for different functions, galas, and trade shows, and signing autographs has always been personally rewarding to me. I meet so many wonderful people who have embraced the movie in their hearts. I feel very privileged to have been chosen to be a part of American film history. People often tell me stories of how the movie has changed their lives or given them new direction. Some have even confessed considering suicide, but watching the movie somehow touched them and gave them a reason to live. I feel the movie has a mission.

As Zuzu I get a lot of strange questions and requests. At autograph signings I am frequently asked to sign things like rose petals (of course), grave items, furniture, dolls, shoes, various angel items, cards, and bells. One excited young man asked me to sign his rear end. It was a tempting offer, but I had to decline! The two questions I am most asked are: "What was it like to work with Mr. Stewart?" and "What happened to the rose petals?"

I have amassed quite a collection of *It's a Wonderful Life* items over the years. I have one room in my house that I call my *It's a Wonderful Life* Room," where I display them. I receive many items, especially angels, from fans I have met and from people that are touched by the film. I have decorated the whole house with angel gifts.

One of the most often asked questions I get is what it was like to work with Frank Capra. Capra was the kind of director who could reach inside and get what he wanted. Most directors would stand next to you and tell you what they wanted, period. Capra would get down on his knees and look at you eye level. He was very gentle and patient with all of us kids.

It's a Wonderful Life has great appeal, even to lawyers! I once got a letter from a lawyer in Missouri, who wanted me to know that he used some excerpts and ideas from the movie for a closing statement in a wrongful-death suit. It was successful, and the person received $700,000 settlement instead of $50,000!

I was shooting *Rio Grande* with John Wayne at the time the Korean conflict broke out. The film was being shot in Moab, Utah, in July, and it was hard to get a plane home because planes were all being used. Mr. Wayne bought $300 worth of fireworks and a huge birthday cake to celebrate my tenth birthday, which was on the Fourth of July.

Bing Crosby was a lot of fun to work with. I worked with him in *Blue Skies*. I played a character named Mary Eliz-

abeth and got to sit on his lap and hear him sing 'Getting Nowhere.' He liked to play practical jokes on the set and laugh a lot. I saw him once when the movie was done, and I told him I got a new dog and named him Bing, because he liked to howl all night. What I didn't know is there was a reporter with him from *Variety* magazine. Sure enough, the next morning the story was in the magazine.

Cary Grant was my all-time favorite to work with. He loved children, and it was quite obvious that he enjoyed being with them. I worked with him in *The Bishop's Wife*, and there was an ice rink built right on the set. He actually ice-skated, and every day at lunch he would come get me and pull me around the rink on a sled.

I have been a wife and mother of seven children. Yes, I was a Mary Bailey for many years! Like so many of you, I also struggled with a full-time job, car pools, involvement in theater, volunteer work, entertaining, etc.—always racing the clock! (Do they give a degree for that?) And yet every night eight hungry mouths expected Betty Crocker to pop out of the kitchen with a home-cooked meal!

Family meals are where we can regain some of the values lost to the high-pressure, hurry-up society we live in. There is a special closeness and togetherness to be found with your loved ones, sharing ideas and experiences while enjoying the taste of a mouth-watering meal.

Perhaps you will enjoy the many luscious creations that are virtually jumping off the page for you to try. Some of my recipes are quick, easy, and delicious. Others may take more time, but all have become family favorites. In the recipe section you will notice a rose next to certain titles to indicate that the recipe is one of my personal favorites.

This book is really all about love. ***Enjoy!***

A Brief History of *It's a Wonderful Life*

It's a Wonderful Life began as a twenty-four-page Christmas pamphlet called *The Greatest Gift.* Writer Philip Van Doren Stern wrote *The Greatest Gift* in 1943, with the hope of selling it to a publisher. That never came to pass, so he had two hundred copies printed up as Christmas cards for his family and friends.

Three months later, RKO Radio Studios saw a copy and bought the story from Van Doren Stern for ten thousand dollars. RKO wanted Cary Grant to play the part of George Pratt, who later became George Bailey. Three scripts were written, but none of the three panned out. Eventually Cary Grant would move on to star in *The Bishop's Wife.*

In 1945, Frank Capra, having served in the Office of Information, was fresh off a tour of duty in World War II. He formed Liberty Films, came across the Van Doren Stern work, and decided that this would be his first postwar commercial film. He purchased the original story and the three previously written scripts for the same ten thousand dollars RKO had paid. Later, RKO would serve as distributor for the film.

Capra changed the name of the film to *It's a Wonderful Life* and hired the married writing team of Albert Hackett and Frances Goodrich to help him develop the final version of the script. He had only one person in mind for the part of George Bailey: Jimmy Stewart. This film would be the third for Stewart and Capra, and also Stewart's first film since returning from the war.

Capra was a stickler for details. He wanted the wintry scenes to look and sound real. Up until that time, movie snow was typically made from corn flakes painted white, which made too much noise when it fell. His snow scenes were created by using 3,000 tons of shaved ice, 300 tons of gypsum, 6,000 gallons of a water-foamite-soap solution, and 300 tons of plaster.

When deciding on a cast for the movie, Capra had several people in mind for every role except George Bailey. For Capra, Jimmy Stewart was the only logical choice. It's amusing today to picture these other Capra ideas:

- Hattie McDaniel as Annie the maid
- W. C. Fields as Uncle Billy
- Olivia DeHavilland as Mary Bailey
- Vincent Price as Henry Potter
- Betty Lawford as Violet Bick
- Cary Grant as George Bailey (before Capra bought the film rights)

Filming began on April 8, 1946, and finished on July 27, 1946. It is estimated that Capra spent nearly three million dollars on the film, and a year after its release it had grossed only $3,300,000.

Despite wide publicity and a few good reviews, the film was panned by most critics and the public. It was nevertheless nominated for five Oscars, including Best Film, Best Actor, and Best Director, but *It's a Wonderful Life* was completely shut out, with the exception of its special-effects team, which won an award for its convincing snow.

CAST

George Bailey, Jimmy Stewart; *Mary Hatch Bailey*, Donna Reed; *Pop Bailey (Peter)*, Samuel S. Hinds; *Ma Bailey*, Beulah Bondi; *Harry Bailey*, Todd Karns; *Uncle Billy*, Thomas Mitchell; *Henry F. Potter*, Lionel Barrymore; *Clarence Oddbody*, Henry Travers; *Mr. Gower*, H. B. Warner; *Sam Wainwright*, Frank Albertson; *Violet Bick*, Gloria Grahame; *Ernie Bishop*, Frank Faylen; *Bert*, Ward Bond; *Ruth Dakin-Bailey*, Virginia Patton; *Cousin Tillie*, Mary Treen; *Cousin Eustace*, Charles Williams; *Mr. Martini*, Bill Edmonds; *Mrs. Martini*, Argentina Brunetti; *Nick the Bartender*, Sheldon Leonard; *Annie*, Lillian Randolph; *Marty Hatch*, Hal Landon; *Mrs. J. W. Hatch*, Sara Edwards; *Peter*

Bailey, Larry Simms; *Janie Bailey,* Carol Coombs; *Zuzu Bailey,* Karolyn Grimes; *Tommy Bailey,* Jimmy Hawkins; *Freddie (at pool),* Carl "Alfalfa" Switzer; *Mickey (with Freddie),* Bobby Scott; *Young George,* Bobbie Anderson; *Young Mary,* Jean Gale; *Young Violet,* Jeanine Ann Roose; *Young Harry,* Georgie Nokes; *Young Marty,* Danny Mummert; *Young Sam,* Ronnie Ralph; *Mr. Welch,* Stanley Andrews; *Mr. Partridge,* Harry Holman; *Dr. Campbell,* Harry Cheshire; *Mr. Carter (bank examiner),* Charles Halton; *Joe (at the luggage shop),* Ray Walker; *Potter's Bodyguard,* Frank Hagney; *Reinman (rent collector),* Charles Lane; *Tom (from Building and Loan),* Edward Keen; *Mrs. Davis,* Ellen Corby; *Man on Porch,* Dick Elliott; *House Owner,* Farrell Macdonald; *Bank Teller,* Ed Featherstone; *Bill Poster,* Gary Owen; *Tollhouse Keeper,* Tom Fadden; *Jane Wainwright,* Marian Carr; *Sheriff,* Al Bridges.

Credits

Producer-director, Frank Capra; assistant director, Arthur S. Black; Writers, Albert Hackett, Frances Goodrich, Frank Capra; additional scenes, Jo Swering; photography, Joseph Walker, Joseph Biroc; film editor, William Hornbeck; art direction, Jack Okey; special effects, Russell Cully; set decorator, Emile Kuri; Sound, John Aalberg, Richard Van Hassen, Clem Portman; music, Dimitri Tiomkin; makeup, Gordon Bau; costumes, Edward Stevenson.

Publicizing *It's a Wonderful Life*

In 1946, movie studios couldn't use the broad array of media available today. Television was still being perfected, so they had to rely on newspaper and magazine ads, billboards, some radio spots, and previews at the local Bijou.

It's a Wonderful Life was advertised in all the popular magazines of its day, including *The Saturday Evening Post, Life, Time,* and *Newsweek.* The Bailey family appeared on the cover of *Newsweek,* December 30, 1946, had a very good review in *Time* on December 23, 1946, and were featured in a beautiful five-page layout in *Life* on December 30, 1946.

Time summarized the movie favorably and quoted Capra as saying that "stars are secondary. Story value will have foremost precedence in production."

Life magazine categorized *It's a Wonderful Life* as a "top-notch comedy":

Director Capra has created a masterful edifice of comedy and sentiment. Except for a few unnecessarily rambunctious moments, James Stewart is excellent in one of the longest movie parts on record. Even after five years away in the Army, he seems the best leading man in pictures.

QUICK FRANK CAPRA FACTS

- He was born in Palermo, Italy, 1897
- Moved to Los Angeles with his family when he was six
- Started as a writer for the Mack Sennett Studio
- Started directing career at Columbia
- Served in World War II and left the army as a colonel
- Formed Liberty Films on April 10, 1945
- *It's a Wonderful Life* was the first Capra film after the war.
- Directed forty-eight films between 1926 and 1961
- Won three Academy Awards for best director
- Died in 1991

Frank Capra and Jimmy Stewart share a hearty laugh on the set.

It's a Wonderful Life Vignettes

It's a Wonderful Life was Jimmy Stewart's first picture since returning from service in World War II. Stewart needed a good vehicle to re-start his career and jumped at the chance to work with Frank Capra again. (This was also Capra's first film since returning from the war.) The film premiered at the Globe Theatre in New York City on December 20, 1946. Unfortunately for both, the film was panned in the United States and in England as too corny!

Although it appeared to be a real city, Bedford Falls was built on four acres at the RKO studio lot in California. One of the longest sets ever created for a movie, it spanned three city blocks and had over seventy storefronts and buildings, including a bank, post office, and library. For realism, Capra had two dozen live oaks planted down the middle of the street.

One of the most frequently debated scenes is the Charleston contest—whether or not the pool beneath the gym floor is real; (George Bailey and Mary Hatch fall in when Carl "Alfalfa" Switzer opens the floor). The pool is real; it really is under the gym floor; and it is still in use today at Beverly Hills High School.

Henry F. Potter, the cantankerous old miser played to perfection by Lionel Barrymore, wasn't part of the original story. He was created by Frank Capra to give the film depth. Another character created by Capra was Uncle Billy's pet raven, Jimmy. Jimmy the raven first appeared in Capra's *You Can't Take It With You*, in 1938. Jimmy appeared in every Capra film after that.

If it was winter out, why isn't people's breath visible? Although a good part of the film has snow in it, there's never any breath mist. Although it looked like Christmas Eve, the film was actually shot during a record-breaking heat wave in 1946. (One time you can see breath mist is in one scene between George Bailey and Violet Bick, which was shot at night.)

About Karolyn Grimes

In the true spirit of George Bailey in *It's a Wonderful Life*, Karolyn Grimes has prevailed over several tragedies. She was born in 1940 and was raised in the heart of the great American film capital, Hollywood, California. Her dad worked long hours in management for Safeway stores, and her mom stayed at home to raise Karolyn, their only child.

When Karolyn was four years old, World War II was raging, and her dad was certain he would soon be drafted. Her mom couldn't bear the thought of being poor and didn't think the family could survive on army pay. So began young Karolyn's acting career. A family friend introduced them to Lola Moore, a well-known Hollywood child talent agent. Karolyn's natural talent was recognized, and after a few interviews she began to get small roles in movies. Ironically, her dad was supposed to go into the Army the same day the war ended!

Karolyn's bright smile and cute curls landed her roles in many top movies with the hottest stars of the era, including *The Bishop's Wife*, with Cary Grant; *Rio Grande*, with John Wayne; and *Blue Skies*, with Bing Crosby, to name a few. However, she is perhaps best loved and remembered for her portrayal of Zuzu Bailey in *It's a Wonderful Life*, with Jimmy Stewart.

Karolyn's career blossomed and soon she was performing on television in the *Ford Theater* drama hour and in commercials. By the age of fifteen, Karolyn had tragically lost both her parents. Her

Karolyn Grimes today.

mother had died from Alzheimer's disease, and her father had been killed in an auto accident. No other family members lived in California, so she was sent to live with relatives in the Midwest—who wanted her to have no part of Hollywood. In true Bailey fashion, Karolyn began to make a new life for herself. After high school she decided to stay in the Midwest instead of returning to Hollywood. She majored in drama and music at Central Missouri State, married, and raised a Bailey-size family of her own.

Although it has been fifty years since *It's a Wonderful Life* was filmed, Karolyn has never been far away from it. She travels the country signing autographs and appearing at charity events with an *It's a Wonderful Life* theme. In 1993, Target Stores reunited Karolyn and the other three "Bailey children" for a tour of the country. They participated in the Hollywood Christmas parade and appeared together on *Entertainment Tonight, Inside Edition*, and the Vicki Lawrence Show, and in *People* magazine. Karolyn performs in regional theater, is active in fine arts organizations, does volunteer work, and has launched a promising new singing career.

Selected Movie Credits

Hans Christian Andersen (Danny Kaye) 1952
The Bishop's Wife (Cary Grant, Loretta Young) 1947
Blue Skies (Bing Crosby, Fred Astaire) 1946
Rio Grande (John Wayne, Maureen O'Hara) 1950
Lust for Gold (Ida Lupino, Glenn Ford) 1949
Honeychile (Judy Canova, Alan Hale, Jr.) 1951
Pardon My Past (Harry Davenport, Fred MacMurray) 1946
That Night With You (Irene Ryan, Buster Keaton) 1945
It's a Wonderful Life (Jimmy Stewart) 1946
The Private Affairs of Bel Ami (Angela Lansbury) 1947
Albuquerque (Randolph Scott, Lon Chaney) 1948
Mother Wore Tights (Betty Grable) 1947
The Jolson Story (Larry Parks, Evelyn Keyes) 1946
Philo Vance's Gamble (Alan Curtis) 1947

The Zuzu Bailey Fan Club

Karolyn Grimes receives fan mail from all around the United States and other parts of the world. People love to write her and express how much *It's a Wonderful Life* has meant to them. Many people write to say how the movie changed their lives or helped them in a crisis. Others send photographs of themselves or their kids who are named Zuzu, in her honor.

The Zuzu Bailey fan club is alive and growing bigger each year. Besides the fan club, there is an info-packed newsletter and a growing number of other terrific items available from *It's A Wonderful Life.* For more information about the Zuzu Bailey Fan Club or merchandise available, write to:

Zuzu Bailey Fan Club Info
P.O. Box 225
Stilwell, KS 66085

Zuzu hopes to hear from you soon!

Recipes

Above: ***George Bailey steals Mary (Donna Reed) from Carl "Alfalfa" Switzer.***

Below: ***Mary Hatch and Harry Bailey share a first kiss***

Appetizers

"It's a Wonderful Life *is my favorite movie for lots of reasons. It was my first film after coming home from World War II. I was excited to be working with Frank Capra again because he had a way of making characters come to life. George Bailey, the character I played, had real values and believed in something. All of this made the film very special to me.*"

—*Jimmy Stewart* (George Bailey)

Ruth Dakin Bailey (Virginia Patton Moss) receives a congratulatory kiss from George Bailey.

Ruth Dakin's Bacon Wraps

Add 1 tablespoon of horseradish to the sauce for extra zip.

2 (6-ounce) cans sliced water chestnuts, drained
1 pound bacon strips cut crosswise in thirds
¼ cup mayonnaise or salad dressing
¼ cup chili sauce
¾ cup dark brown sugar

WATER CHESTNUTS

Preheat oven to 350 degrees F. Wrap one or two water chestnut slices in each piece of bacon, inserting a toothpick through each to hold the bacon in place. Bake on a cookie sheet in preheated oven until bacon is crisp, about 30 to 40 minutes.

SAUCE

Mix mayonnaise, chili sauce, and brown sugar together, blend well, and chill until bacon wraps are done. Arrange bacon wraps around bowl of dipping sauce on a platter and serve.

45 to 50 hors d'oeuvres

I Love You Truly Artichoke Heart Dip

1 (6-ounce) jar marinated artichoke hearts
½ cup mayonnaise or salad dressing
2 tablespoons minced onion
Salt, pepper, Cayenne pepper to taste
2 crisp-cooked slices bacon, crumbled

Chop artichokes in blender. Add remaining ingredients and blend. Pour into serving dish and chill. Great with raw vegetables and crackers. For extra effect and taste, spoon dip into a small hollowed-out loaf of bread.

About 4 servings

Q. How old was George Bailey in
a. 1919 b.1928 c.1946?

Martini's Fiesta Olive Spread

1 (6-ounce) can black olives, drained and chopped fine
1 cup shredded Cheddar cheese
1 teaspoon Worcestershire sauce
¼ teaspoon curry powder
7 tablespoons mayonnaise
1 tablespoon finely chopped green onion
1 mini loaf rye or pumpernickel bread, sliced thin

Preheat oven to 350 degrees F. Mix olives, cheese, Worcestershire, curry powder, mayonnaise, and green onion and spread on mini bread slices. Bake in preheated oven until bubbly, about 10 minutes.

About 2 cups

Auld Lang Syne Cheesy Fruit and Nut Spread

3–4 tablespoons honey
1 tablespoon apple schnapps or apple brandy
8 ounces cream cheese, softened
½ cup dried apple chunks, chopped fine
¼ cup finely chopped toasted almonds
¼ cup sliced almonds

Gradually blend honey and schnapps or brandy with cream cheese, until well blended. Stir in apples and chopped almonds. Scatter the sliced almonds on top of mixture, cover, and chill for 3 to 4 hours.

Best served with whole-grain crackers, sliced apples or pears, and celery.

About 1½ cups

***A:** a. 12; b. 21; c. 39.*

Violet Bick's Devilish Eggs

5 eggs
⅓ cup mayonnaise
2 tablespoons prepared mustard
2 tablespoons finely chopped onion
Dash of pepper
Paprika to taste

Place eggs in 2-quart saucepan, cover with water, and bring to a boil. Reduce heat slightly and boil for 8 to 9 minutes. Remove from heat, place in sink, and run cold water in saucepan until eggs feel cool to the touch. Crack and peel eggs. Cut the eggs in halves lengthwise. Remove the yolks and set the empty white halves aside. Place the yolks in a medium mixing bowl. Mash the yolks, then mix in the mayonnaise, mustard, onion, and pepper. Carefully spoon the yolk mixture into the empty egg halves. Arrange on serving plate, sprinkle with paprika, and add a celery leaf garnish. *2 or 3 tablespoons of finely chopped ham can be added for still more flavor. For extra zip, use honey mustard or Dijon mustard.*

10 servings

Hammy Sammy Wainwright Roll-ups

⅓ cup finely chopped green onions, with green tops
8 ounces cream cheese, at room temperature
8 slices Polish ham, or your favorite ham, sliced medium-thick

Mix green onions with cream cheese. Spread mixture over each ham slice. Roll ham slices and cut into bite-size circles. *Pineapple cream cheese is also good with this recipe.*

32 hors d'oeuvres

Q: Which of George's ears was bad?

Crabby Potter's Cheesy Muffins

2 cups shredded Cheddar or Monterey Jack cheese
⅓ cup butter or margarine
¼ cup milk
¼ cup coarsely grated carrot
1 (8-ounce) can of crab meat, drained and shredded
6 English muffins or onion bagels, split

Preheat broiler. Heat cheese, butter, and milk in a saucepan over low heat, stirring until melted and well blended. Simmer, stirring occasionally until it thickens a bit. Stir in grated carrot and crab meat. Spread English muffins or bagels with cheese-crab mixture and place, split side up, on an oven rack in broiler pan. Broil until slightly brown, about 2 minutes, depending on how high broiler rack is placed.

12 servings

Potter the Crab Cakes

4 slices whole wheat or white bread
12 ounces crab meat, drained and shredded or finely chopped
2 eggs
1 tablespoon Worcestershire sauce
3 tablespoons coarsely grated carrot
1 teaspoon dry mustard
½ teaspoon salt
¼ teaspoon pepper
2 tablespoons vegetable oil

Remove crusts from bread and cut into tiny pieces. Mix bread, crab meat, eggs, Worcestershire sauce, grated carrot, mustard, salt, and pepper. Roll mixture into 8 balls and flatten into patties. Heat oil in a large skillet and fry patties over medium heat until golden brown on each side.

Great with cocktail or tartar sauce.

8 servings

***A:** The left one.*

Violet Bick's Sweet Potato Puffs

4 medium sweet potatoes
⅓ cup finely chopped broccoli florets
2 tablespoons butter or margarine
Salt and pepper to taste
1 package ready-to-bake pastry dough or crescent roll dough

Preheat oven to 400 degrees F. Wash and cut small slits in one side of sweet potatoes. Microwave sweet potatoes together for 6 minutes on HIGH setting. After microwaving, bake sweet potatoes in preheated oven for 15 minutes, or until very tender. Remove from oven and cut in halves lengthwise. Carefully scoop out insides and discard skins. Mash sweet potatoes and add broccoli, butter, salt, and pepper.

Lower oven temperature to 350 degrees F. If using ready-to-bake pastry dough, cut into triangle shapes big enough to accommodate filling. If using ready-to-bake crescent roll dough, separate into triangle shapes. Place triangle shapes on pastry mat and place equal amounts of filling on triangles. Take ends of dough and wrap over top, pinching together. Arrange puffs about an inch apart on ungreased cookie sheet and bake until golden brown, about 10 to 15 minutes, checking frequently.

8 to 10 servings

Ma Bailey's Holiday Spinach Delight

1 (10-ounce) package frozen spinach, thawed and drained
1 cup mayonnaise
¾ cup sour cream
1 small package ranch or Hidden Valley salad dressing mix
1 clove garlic, chopped fine
½ small onion, chopped fine
Salt and pepper to taste

In a large mixing bowl, combine all ingredients; mix well. Chill and serve with favorite crackers, bread sticks, or torn pieces of French bread.

10 to 12 servings

Q: What organization did George belong to as a young man?

Sam Wainwright's Broccoli Hee-Haw Surprise

1 (8-ounce) package frozen puff pastry
1 tablespoon butter or margarine
½ pound fresh mushrooms, chopped
Salt and pepper to taste
1 clove fresh garlic, minced
2 cups finely chopped fresh broccoli florets
1 cup shredded Swiss cheese

Let pastry thaw for 30 minutes at room temperature. Heat butter in medium skillet over medium heat and sauté mushrooms and garlic; add salt and pepper to taste. Add broccoli, cook 3 more minutes. Remove mixture from heat.

Preheat oven to 400 degrees F. Lightly grease a 10×12-inch baking pan or small pizza pan. Unfold pastry onto pan and pour mixture on top. Cover with cheese and bake in preheated oven for 20 minutes, or until golden brown. Cut into squares and serve.

10 to 12 servings

Mr. Martini's Midnight Snack Marinara Sticks

1 medium onion, chopped fine
2 cloves garlic, chopped fine
¼ cup virgin olive oil
3 cups tomato sauce
2 tablespoons chopped fresh parsley
½ tablespoon dried basil
½ tablespoon dried oregano
Salt and pepper to taste
1 package soft bread sticks, English muffins, or onion bagels (or more than 1 package, depending on size)
2 cups shredded mozzarella cheese (about)

In a medium saucepan, sauté onion and garlic in olive oil. Add tomato sauce, parsley, basil, oregano, salt, and pepper. Simmer sauce over low heat, uncovered, for 1 hour, stirring occasionally.

***A:** The National Geographic Society.*

Preheat broiler. When sauce is done, arrange bread sticks or English muffins on an ungreased cookie sheet. Sprinkle enough mozzarella cheese to cover. Broil on middle rack until cheese is melted and bubbly, about 2 minutes. Remove and serve with sauce on top, or on the side, as a dip. *Extra sauce is also good the second day with pasta.*

12 servings

Spicy Bean Dip

This is a favorite recipe of Todd Karns, who played Harry Bailey in the film. Todd is an artist and lives with his wife, Kate, in Mexico.

2 (16-ounce) cans refried beans (fat-free if possible)
1 medium onion, chopped fine
2 cups Cheddar cheese
1 cup sour cream
½ head iceberg lettuce, shredded
½ green bell pepper, diced
1 small tomato, diced
1 (16-ounce) bottle of your favorite hot salsa
Tabasco sauce to taste (optional)
1 bag of your favorite tortilla chips

In a medium saucepan, over medium heat, cook beans and onion together until well warmed. Spoon the mixture into a 9×12×2-inch casserole dish. Layer half the cheese on top of the beans. In layers, add sour cream, lettuce, green pepper, tomato, remaining cheese, and salsa. Dip with tortilla chips. Can be served warm or cold.

6 to 8 servings

Q: What were George's three favorite sounds?

Bedford Falls Party Time Favorite Cheese Ball

2 (8-ounce) tubs cream cheese with pineapple chunks
1 cup shredded Cheddar cheese
2 tablespoons finely chopped red onion
2 slices ham, chopped fine
½ teaspoon garlic powder
2 tablespoons green bell pepper, finely chopped
1 cup pecans, chopped

Let cream cheese soften at room temperature for a couple of hours. In a large bowl, mix all ingredients except the pecans; cover with plastic wrap, and chill for 1 hour. Form cheese mixture into ball and roll in pecans. Serve with your favorite crackers or veggies.

12 to 16 servings

Cousin Tillie's Saucy Meatballs

2 pounds ground sirloin
3 eggs
1 (1-ounce) package dry onion soup mix
1 cup dried bread crumbs
Salt and pepper to taste
Vegetable oil
2 (10¾-ounce) cans condensed cream of mushroom soup

Preheat oven to 350 degrees F. In a large mixing bowl, combine ground sirloin, eggs, soup mix, bread crumbs, and salt and pepper. Shape into 1-inch balls. Cover a large skillet with a thin coating of vegetable oil and brown meatballs, in batches on all sides over medium heat. Drain and place in 3 quart casserole dish. Pour cream of mushroom soup over top, making sure each meat ball is moist. Add more seasonings if desired. Bake in preheated oven for about 30 minutes. Serve alone or over cooked noodles.

8 servings

***A:** Anchor chains, plane motors, and train whistles.*

Martini's Happy Hour Sausage-Mushroom Treat

1 pound large fresh mushrooms
1 pound fresh sausage
1 clove garlic, chopped fine
2 tablespoons butter or margarine
3 cups shredded mozzarella

Preheat oven to 350 degrees F. Remove all mushroom stems, wash, and let dry. Hollow out caps with small spoon. In a large skillet, over medium heat, brown sausage and garlic. Drain well and let stand. Finely chop mushroom stems. Sauté in butter in a medium skillet over medium heat until tender. Add sausage and cheese and cook over low heat until cheese is melted, about 3 to 5 minutes. Place mushroom caps in a shallow baking dish and fill with sausage mixture. Bake in preheated oven until mushrooms and cheese are lightly browned, about 8 to 10 minutes. *Any left-over mixture goes great in omelets the next morning.*

About 16 hors d'oeuvres

Well-wishers give George and Mary a proper wedding send-off. (At the couple's left, Mrs. Hatch is still sad that daughter Mary married a Bailey!)

Beverages

"It's a Wonderful Life *is as addicting as any drug! Once you start watching it, you get caught up, and one scene leads to another. Then before you know it, the movie is over. My favorite character is Clarence, but the best scene, and perhaps the greatest love scene ever filmed, is when George and Mary are on the phone to Sam "Hee-Haw" Wainwright. You can actually feel the electricity!"*

—*Jimmy Hawkins* (Tommy Bailey)

George Bailey thinks angel Clarence Oddbody doesn't exist.

Clarence Oddbody's Old-Fashioned Mulled Cider

The rose water called for in this recipe is available at most gourmet food shops.

- 3 quarts natural cider
- 8 whole cloves
- 1 whole nutmeg
- 2 cinnamon sticks
- ½ cup dark brown sugar
- 2 drops rose water (optional)

Put all ingredients in a large pot, bring to a boil over medium heat, and simmer for 15 minutes. Strain and serve in warmed glasses or noggins.

16 6-ounce servings

Cousin Tillie's Fruity-Fizz Punch

- 8 cups 7-Up or ginger ale
- 8 cups cranberry-apple juice
- 1 (6-ounce) can frozen orange juice concentrate
- 1 (8-ounce) can lemon juice
- 1 (8-ounce) can sliced pineapple
- 1 orange, sliced

In a large punch bowl, combine 7-Up and cranberry-apple juice. Add frozen orange and lemon juice and stir until completely dissolved. Add juice from can of pineapple. Float pineapple and orange slices on top. Chill before serving or serve over ice.

18 8-ounce servings

Q: What did George do when he couldn't open the gate at Mary's house when he visited her one night?

J. W. Hatch's Sourpuss Home-Style Lemonade

6 large lemons, at room temperature
1 cup sugar
1½ cups boiling water
8 cups cold water
1 lemon, sliced

Roll all lemons until soft to the touch. Cut lemons in half and squeeze out juice into a bowl. Strain into a large pitcher and add sugar. Place all lemon rinds in bowl and pour boiling water over them; let stand until cool. Strain rind juice into pitcher and add cold water. Stir well. Chill and serve over ice with a slice of lemon on edge of glass.

9 to 10 servings

Old Man Gower's Early Riser (With a Kick)

Orange juice as desired, per glass
2 shots of champagne
1 small dash of Tabasco sauce

Combine all ingredients in a tall glass and stir. *Don't guzzle!*

1 serving

Violet Bick's Spicy Tea

2 quarts water
5 heaping teaspoons instant tea
1 cup sugar
5 tablespoons lemon juice
1 teaspoon vanilla extract
1 teaspoon almond extract
½ teaspoon ground allspice

***A:** He kicked the gate open.*

In a large saucepan, bring water to a boil and add instant tea. Pour tea into a large pitcher and add all the other ingredients. Stir well. Can be served hot or chilled.

8 8-ounce servings

Bedford Falls Ladies' Auxiliary Peppermint Tea

2 quarts water
5 heaping teaspoons instant tea
¾ cup sugar
1 teaspoon peppermint extract, or more
1 lemon, sliced

In a large saucepan, bring water to a boil and add instant tea. Pour tea into a large pitcher and add sugar; stir well. Add peppermint extract and stir. More extract can be added for a more minty taste. Garnish glasses with lemon slices.

8 8-ounce servings

Nick's Get-You-There-Quick Iced Lemony Bourbon

1 (6-ounce) can frozen lemonade concentrate
6 ounces orange juice (prepared, not concentrate)
1 tablespoon lime juice
6 ounces Bourbon

Scoop out frozen lemonade concentrate into a blender container, saving the can. Use the lemonade can to measure 6 ounces orange juice and 6 ounces Bourbon; add to blender container. Add lime juice and enough ice to fill container. Blend until smooth. Freeze until 10 to 15 minutes before serving.

4 to 6 servings

Q: How much was George making when he was twenty-eight?

Moon Glow Romance Hot Apple Cider

Freshly made apple cider
1 clove
Pinch of brown sugar
Pinch of ground allspice
Cinnamon stick

Purchase some fresh apple cider from your favorite apple orchard. Fill a big mug with apple cider. Add clove, brown sugar, and allspice; stir. Put in cinnamon stick and heat mix in microwave to desired temperature (about 1 to 1½ minutes on HIGH.) *For extra zip, add a shot of apple schnapps.*

1 serving

George and Mary's Wedding Day Cocktail Punch

3 cups chopped honeydew melon
3 cups chopped cantaloupe
2½ cups orange juice
⅓ cup fresh lime juice
4 tablespoons honey
2 cups dry champagne
Mint leaves or orange slices for garnish

Put honeydew and cantaloupe in blender container. Add all the other ingredients and blend on low speed until smooth. Pour in glasses and garnish with mint leaves or orange slices.

8 to 10 servings

Billy Bailey's Irish Coffee

1 mug coffee
Sugar, as desired
1 shot Bailey's Irish Cream
Whipped cream

A: George made the whopping sum of $45 per week!

Prepare a mug of your favorite coffee—do not fill too full. Add desired sugar and Bailey's Irish Cream; stir. Top with a generous dollop of whipped cream. *Don't guzzle! For a real treat, add a shot of Grand Marnier.*

1 serving

Peter Bailey's Traditional Family Eggnog

Eggnog has been a favorite holiday beverage for centuries. Today's eggnog is a descendent of the centuries-old English brew "sack posset," a hot drink made of rum, ale, eggs, and milk. It became especially popular during the cold months when fresh fruit juices weren't available. These recipes should delight and warm you up!

VERSION ONE

Fill your favorite mug or glass three-quarters full with your favorite eggnog. Stir in one shot of fine cognac or brandy and two pinches of ground nutmeg. Sprinkle nutmeg on top and enjoy.

VERSION TWO

For a spicier taste, substitute rum for cognac or brandy, and sprinkle with ground cinnamon.

VERSION THREE

For a nonalcoholic treat, substitute a few drops rum or almond extract for liquor.

Each version makes 1 serving

Uncle Billy's New Year's Eve Hot Buttered Rumble

BASE

½ cup butter
1 cup dark brown sugar, packed
⅓ teaspoon ground cloves
⅓ teaspoon ground cinnamon

Q: What was George's job during World War II?

In a medium mixing bowl, cream butter, sugar, and spices until mixture is very smooth and fluffy.

DRINK

Dark rum, to taste
Boiling water
Cinnamon sticks

Put 2 tablespoons of base mixture in a large mug. Add one or two shots of dark rum. Fill mug with boiling water and stir. Add a cinnamon stick for extra flavor.

If you wish to store leftover base, it will keep for 5 to 7 days in a tightly covered container in refrigerator.

Makes enough base for 12 to 16 servings

Bailey Kids' Imitation Hot Buttered Rumble

BASE

1 pound butter or margarine, at room temperature
2 pounds dark brown sugar
2 pounds confectioner's sugar
1 quart vanilla ice cream

In a large mixing bowl, combine butter and sugars; cream until very smooth. Add ice cream, 1 cup at a time, mixing in each addition well.

DRINK

Boiling water
Almond or rum extract
Cinnamon sticks

In a large mug, put 2 teaspoons creamy mixture and add boiling water. Add ½ teaspoon almond or rum extract and stir. *Add cinnamon stick and enjoy!*

Makes enough base for 24 servings

***A:** George served as air raid warden, and he was in charge of paper, scrap, and rubber drives.*

Clarence Oddbody's Heavenly Hot Mulled Wine

What Clarence Ordered at Nick's Place!

5 cups burgundy wine
5 cups fresh apple cider
⅓ cup dark brown sugar
3 cinnamon sticks
10 whole cloves
1 pinch ground allspice
Orange slices for garnish (optional)

In a large saucepan, combine all ingredients and stir well. Heat to desired temperature, stirring occasionally. Serve in coffee mugs or similar glasses. Garnish with orange slices if you wish.

8 to 10 servings

Mr. Gower's Help-Ya-Get-To-Sleep-Fast Hot Chocolate Mint Toddy

Can be served with whipped cream on top. For a little kick, substitute 1 shot peppermint schnapps for extract.

Hot chocolate mix
Peppermint extract or miniature candy cane
Whipped cream (optional)

Prepare a mug of your favorite hot chocolate and add one drop of peppermint extract, or more if you like, and stir. Use miniature candy cane if you want, in place of extract.

1 serving

George is humiliated by laughter when a crowd gathers and hears him talking romantic nonsense to Violet Bick (Gloria Grahame).

Nick the Bartender (Sheldon Leonard) and Mr. Martini (Bill Edmonds) help George up after he's been punched by Mr. Welch (Stanley Andrews).

Soups

"Capra was so into the entire picture! He seemed to live each moment as it was being acted out, laughing or crying with the mood of the scene. I remember watching him very closely during the filming of the last scene. He was mouthing the words of every line with all the sentiment of the actors, and tears were rolling down his face. I think he truly believed in the film and the premise that guardian angels really do exist."

—*Argentina Brunetti* (Mrs. Martini)

Jimmy Stewart and Donna Reed pose for a publicity photo.

George and Mary's Spring Fling Vegetable Soup

1 small onion, sliced and separated into rings
3–4 stalks celery, chopped
1 tablespoon dried chopped parsley
1 tablespoon butter or margarine
8 cups chicken broth
¼ green bell pepper, chopped
1 cup shredded cabbage
3 medium potatoes, peeled and sliced
2 medium carrots, peeled and sliced

In a heavy soup pot, over medium heat, sauté onion, celery, and parsley in butter, but do not brown. Prepare chicken broth as directed on package and pour into pot. Add all other ingredients and season to taste. Bring to a boil. Reduce heat and cook, covered, for about 40 minutes, until vegetables are tender. Can be served with noodles if desired.

8 servings

Commander Harry Bailey's Navy Bean Soup

2 cups dried navy beans
3 quarts water
1 medium ham bone
2 cups chopped celery
1 cup finely chopped onion
3 medium tomatoes, cut into bite-size pieces
3 medium potatoes, peeled and diced
Salt and pepper to taste
1 tablespoon chopped parsley

In a large bowl, soak navy beans in water to cover by 2 inches overnight; drain before cooking. In a large soup pot, add beans, 2 quarts water, and ham bone; bring to a boil. Reduce heat and simmer, covered, until beans are soft, stirring occasionally. Add all vegetables, seasonings, and parsley, and simmer for 30 minutes, or until tender. *Tastes great with corn bread or fresh rolls.*

6 to 8 servings

Q: Who punched George, and where did he get hit?

Potter's Full-of-Hot-Air Black Bean Soup

1 pound dried black beans
8 cups water
1 medium onion, chopped fine
2 cloves garlic, minced
4 tablespoons butter
2 celery stalks, chopped
1 ham bone
Salt and pepper to taste
½ teaspoon cayenne

Wash beans well. In a large saucepan place 8 cups water. Bring to a boil and add beans. Boil for 5 minutes. Remove from heat, cover, and let stand for 1 hour. Drain and put in a large Dutch oven.

In a skillet, sauté onion and garlic over medium heat in butter; be careful not to burn. Place mixture in a Dutch oven. Add 8 cups water, celery, ham bone, salt, pepper, and cayenne. Cover and bring to a boil. Reduce heat and simmer for 3 hours, stirring occasionally. Remove ham bone. Pour contents of Dutch oven into food processor and puree. Return mixture to Dutch oven. Add more water if mixture seems too thick. Bring to a boil, adding any other seasonings you like. *Tastes great with corn bread.*

8 to 10 servings

Franklin and Joseph's Angelic Cheese Soup

1 cup diced carrots
1 cup diced celery
6 tablespoons butter or margarine
1 cup finely chopped onion
½ cup flour
2½ tablespoons cornstarch
1 (32-ounce) can chicken broth
1 broth can of milk
¼ teaspoon baking soda
Salt and pepper to taste

***A:** Mr. Welch punched George on the left side of the jaw and split his lip.*

1 cup of finely chopped ham
½ teaspoon paprika
1½ cups shredded sharp Cheddar cheese
1 tablespoon chopped parsley

In a medium saucepan, cook carrots and celery in water until tender; drain. In a large soup pot, over medium heat, melt butter and sauté onion until tender, but not brown. Stir in flour and cornstarch, then add broth and milk. Stir until smooth and saucy. Add all other ingredients and simmer until cheese is melted and well blended. *Great with grilled cheese sandwiches or your favorite crackers.*

6 to 8 servings

Stockholders' Thrifty One-Pot Hamburger Soup

1 pound ground sirloin
1 (10¾-ounce) can condensed cream of potato soup
1 (10¾-ounce) can condensed cream of celery soup
3 soup cans milk
2 cups cooked white rice or wild rice
2 medium carrots, diced
1½ cups shredded Cheddar cheese
¾ teaspoon garlic powder
Dried parsley to taste
Salt and pepper to taste

In a large soup pot, brown sirloin. Add soups, milk, and all other ingredients. Cook over medium heat until cheese melts and mixture is well blended. *Makes a complete meal when served with a hot loaf of bread.*

6 servings

Q: What was the last thing George said in the movie?

Cousin Tillie's Bean Counter Chili

1 pound ground round
1 (16-ounce) can cooked tomatoes
1 (8-ounce) can tomato sauce
½ cup finely chopped onion
½ cup finely chopped green bell pepper
1 tablespoon salt
½ teaspoon pepper
3 teaspoons chili powder
¾ teaspoon paprika
Pinch of oregano
2 ½ cups canned or cooked kidney beans, drained

In a large saucepan or Dutch oven, brown sirloin. Add tomatoes, tomato sauce, onion, green bell pepper, salt, pepper, chili powder, paprika, and oregano; stir. Bring to a slow boil. Reduce heat and simmer, covered, for 30 minutes, stirring occasionally. Add kidney beans and cook an additional 45 minutes, stirring frequently. If mixture is too thin, add ½ teaspoon of flour until desired thickness. *Great during football season!*

6 servings

Mrs. Bailey's Fancy New England Clam Chowder

1 tablespoon butter or margarine
½ cup finely chopped onion
¼ cup diced ham
2 (8-ounce) cans minced clams
1 cup finely chopped potato
½ teaspoon salt
Pepper to taste
2 cups milk

A: *"Attaboy, Clarence!"*

In a 2-quart saucepan, melt butter and sauté onion and ham until tender (do not brown). Drain clams, reserving all liquid in a measuring cup. Add water as necessary to make 1 cup. Stir in clams, liquid, potato, salt, and pepper into onion mixture. Bring to a boil. Reduce heat and simmer, covered, until potato is tender, about 10 minutes. Stir in milk and heat thoroughly over medium heat, stirring occasionally.

4 to 6 servings

Sailing on a Cattle Boat Beefy Vegetable Soup

2 tablespoons butter or margarine
1 pound stewing beef, cut into bite-size pieces
2 cups water
1 beef bouillon cube
1½ teaspoons salt
¼ teaspoon pepper
1 bay leaf (optional)
5 cups water
3 medium carrots, sliced
3–4 medium potatoes, peeled and cut into bite-size pieces
2 stalks celery, sliced
1 medium onion, cut into eighths
1 (16-ounce) can whole tomatoes
¼ small head of cabbage, coarsely chopped

In a 4-quart Dutch oven, melt butter and brown beef. Stir in 2 cups water, bouillon, salt, pepper, and bay leaf. Bring to a boil. Reduce heat and simmer, covered, for 1½ hours, stirring occasionally. (Add more water if all water boils out.) Stir in 5 cups of water and all other ingredients; bring to a boil. Reduce heat and simmer, covered, for 1 hour, or until all vegetables are tender. *Serve over cooked noodles with a hot loaf of bread.*

6 servings

Q: As a kid, what did Mary Bailey do to Violet Bick as she walked by her inside Mr. Gower's Drug Store?

Ma Bailey's Come to Sunday Dinner Stew

2 tablespoons butter or margarine
1 pound stewing beef, cut into bite-size pieces
2 cups water
1 beef bouillon cube
1½ teaspoons salt
¼ teaspoon pepper
1 (16-ounce) can tomato sauce
3 cups water
3–4 medium potatoes, cut into bite-size pieces
2 stalks celery, sliced
1 tomato, cut into eighths
1 (10-ounce) bag frozen mixed vegetables
Cornstarch as needed

In a 4-quart Dutch oven, over medium heat, melt butter and brown beef. Add 2 cups water, bouillon, salt, and pepper, and bring to a boil. Reduce heat and simmer, covered, for 1½ hours, stirring occasionally. Add all other ingredients except cornstarch. Bring to a boil. Reduce heat and simmer, covered, for 1 hour, stirring occasionally. Thicken by mixing 2 tablespoons of cornstarch in water and slowly stirring into stew until desired thickness is reached.

6 servings

Peter Bailey's Vegetarian Delight

2 (12-ounce) cans vegetable juice cocktail
2 cups water
1 (8-ounce) can tomato sauce
1 small head cabbage, finely chopped
1 large onion, cut into eighths
3 medium carrots, sliced
2 stalks celery, sliced
1 beef bouillon cube
3 medium potatoes, peeled and cut into bite-size pieces
Salt and pepper to taste

***A:** She stuck her tongue out at her.*

In a 4-quart Dutch oven, place all ingredients and bring to a boil over medium heat. Reduce heat and simmer, covered, for 1 hour, stirring occasionally. *Great with saltines or oyster crackers.*

4 servings

Potter's Cold-as-a-Potato Soup

6 medium leeks
4 tablespoons butter or margarine
4 cups chicken broth
2 large potatoes, peeled and diced
1 cup sour cream
Salt and pepper to taste
Parsley sprigs or celery leaves for garnish

Remove the outer layers and green tops of the leeks, and split. Wash the split leeks well and slice very thin. In a large skillet, sauté the leeks over medium heat in butter, stirring occasionally, until tender, about 5 minutes. In a suitable pot, combine leeks, chicken broth, and potatoes. Bring to a boil. Reduce heat and simmer, covered, for approximately 40 minutes, until tender, stirring occasionally. Strain and reserve broth. Put all vegetables in a blender container and puree until smooth. Add broth and blend until smooth. Put in a large bowl, cover with plastic wrap, and refrigerate for 24 hours. Before serving, stir in sour cream, salt, and pepper. Garnish with parsley sprigs or celery leaves.

6 servings

Q: What did young Mary whisper in George's bad ear at Gower's?

Boardinghouse Steak Soup

2 pounds ground sirloin
¾ cup butter or margarine
1 cup all-purpose flour
2 quarts warm water
1 cup diced onion
1 cup diced carrots
1 cup diced celery
1 (10-ounce) package frozen mixed vegetables
1 (16-ounce) can tomatoes
3 beef bouillon cubes, dissolved in 1 cup of boiling water
Salt and pepper to taste

In a skillet, over medium heat, brown sirloin, drain, and set aside. In a large pot, over medium heat, melt butter and stir in flour to make a smooth base. Gradually stir in water, stirring constantly. Add meat to soup. Add onion, carrots, celery, and mixed vegetables to soup. Bring to a boil. Reduce heat and simmer, covered, for 10 minutes. Add tomatoes, dissolved bouillon, and salt and pepper; bring to a boil. Reduce heat and simmer, covered, for 45 minutes, stirring occasionally. Add other herbs, dried oregano or dried parsley to taste, if desired.

8 to 10 servings

Mrs. Davis's Gentle Lentil Soup

1 pound lentils
1 ham bone
1 teaspoon salt
Pepper to taste
8 cups water
2 tablespoons butter or margarine
2 tablespoons flour
½ teaspoon paprika
1 cup cold water

***A:** She leaned over the counter and said, "George Bailey, I'll love you till the day I die."*

Wash lentils well. Put lentils, ham bone, salt, pepper, and 8 cups water in a soup pot, and bring to a boil. Reduce heat and simmer, covered, for 45 minutes. In a skillet, over medium heat, melt butter. Stir in flour and paprika and brown well. Reduce heat, add cold water, stir well, and cook until thick. Add flour mixture to lentils; stir. Simmer, covered, for 20 minutes, stirring occasionally.

8 to 10 servings

"Oh, Those Rockefellers" Oyster Soup

1 medium onion, chopped fine
½ small green bell pepper, chopped
2 tablespoons butter or margarine
2 cups milk
1 (3-ounce) package cream cheese, at room temperature
1 pint fresh oysters, drained
2 cups chicken broth
Salt and pepper to taste

In a large kettle, over medium heat, sauté onion and green pepper in butter until tender. Add milk and cream cheese. Cook over low heat, about 10 minutes, until mixture is smooth, stirring occasionally. Add oysters, broth, and salt and pepper. Simmer for about 10 minutes, or until oyster edges begin to curl. *Serve with, what else, oyster crackers.*

6 servings

Q: Where did Mary hide when her robe accidentally came off?

Stick-to-the-Ribs U.S.O. Chicken-Potato Soup

1 medium onion, chopped fine
1 small sweet red bell pepper, cleaned, trimmed, and chopped
2 celery stalks, sliced thin
2 tablespoons butter or margarine
1 clove garlic, chopped fine
3 large potatoes, peeled and diced
2 carrots, sliced
1 tomato, diced
3 pounds mixed individual chicken parts, cleaned (remove excess fat, but not skin)
½ teaspoon thyme
Salt and pepper to taste
7 cups water
Shredded Cheddar cheese for garnish

In a large soup pot, over medium heat, sauté onion, bell pepper, and celery in butter until very tender, about 5–7 minutes. Mix in garlic, potatoes, carrots, and tomato. Add chicken pieces and seasonings. Add 7 cups water and bring to a boil. Reduce heat and simmer, covered, for 2 hours.

Take out chicken pieces from soup. Remove meat from bones and cut into pieces. (Discard bones.) Skim as much surface fat from the soup as possible. With a slotted spoon, take about 2 cups of vegetables from the soup and puree in a blender. Return puree to soup along with chicken pieces. Simmer until heated to desired temperature, stirring occasionally. Serve in bowls with Cheddar cheese sprinkled on top. Adjust seasonings to your liking.

8 to 10 servings

***A:** She hid in the hydrangea bushes.*

Sauces

"Frequently I am asked if I really cried in the scene where George Bailey yells at me to play the piano. Yes, definitely! *Mr. Stewart was so convincing. He yelled at me so realistically it was impossible not to cry. It's also no wonder that he cried in the scene while listening to my bad playing. It hasn't improved much either!"*

—*Carol Coombs Mueller* (Janie Bailey)

Director Capra and stars contemplate the famous robe scene, a bit racy for its time.

George toys with the idea of refusing to return Mary's robe.

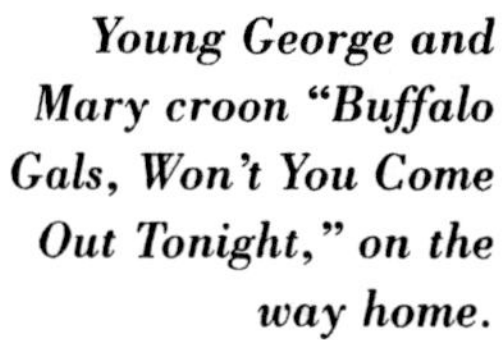

Young George and Mary croon "Buffalo Gals, Won't You Come Out Tonight," on the way home.

Fresh Christmas Cranberry Sauce

½ cup water
½ cup sugar
¼ teaspoon ground cloves
½ teaspoon cinnamon
¼ teaspoon nutmeg
4 cups cranberries, washed
2 tablespoons lemon juice

In a medium saucepan, over medium heat, combine water, sugar, and all the spices, and bring to a boil. Reduce heat and slow-boil for 7 minutes. Add cranberries and lemon juice. Bring to a boil and cook 5 minutes, until cranberry skins split. *Excellent for glazing or dipping. Can also be served cold.*

6 to 8 servings

"Potter the Big Cheese" Sauce

2 tablespoons butter
2 tablespoons flour
1 cup milk
1 cup shredded Cheddar cheese

In a saucepan, over medium heat, melt butter and add flour; blend. Add milk and cook over low heat until mixture is thick, stirring constantly. Add cheese and stir constantly until it is completely melted. Serve hot. *Goes great over vegetables, potatoes, and thick bread or toast.*

Makes 1½ to 2 cups

Q: What did Mary have on the art easel when George came to visit her one night?

Reinmann the Rent Collector's Creamed Spinach Sauce

1½ pounds fresh spinach
Water as needed to cover spinach
1 small onion, chopped fine
1 clove garlic, chopped fine
1 tablespoon chopped parsley
1 tablespoon butter or margarine
1–2 tablespoons flour
Salt and pepper to taste
Milk as needed

Wash spinach well and drain off excess water. In a Dutch oven, over medium heat, add water and spinach and cook, covered, until tender, about 10 minutes. Drain spinach. Cut off and discard any tough stems and mash spinach with a fork until very fine. In a medium saucepan, sauté onion, garlic, and parsley in butter. Gradually add in flour and cook until golden brown, stirring constantly. Add spinach, salt and pepper, and enough milk to make a smooth sauce. *This is terrific over boiled potatoes or pork dishes.*

About 1½ cups

Mrs. Martini's "Old Country" Pesto

½ cup olive oil
1½ garlic cloves, minced
4 tablespoons minced parsley
4 tablespoons grated Parmesan cheese
1 teaspoon dried oregano
Salt and pepper to taste
4 tablespoons pine nuts, chopped fine
4 cups chopped fresh basil

Combine all ingredients in a blender; blend at medium-high speed until sauce is smooth. Pour over your favorite pasta or use as a dip with bread sticks.

Makes about 2 cups

***A:** A drawing of George Bailey lassoing the moon.*

Victory Garden Tomato Sauce

1 teaspoon grated onion
1 tablespoon butter
2 tablespoons flour
1 cup tomato sauce
Salt and pepper to taste
¼ teaspoon oregano

In a saucepan, over medium heat, brown onion in butter. Add flour and blend well. Add tomato sauce, salt and pepper, and oregano. Cook until thick, stirring constantly. *This is good over mashed potatoes, veal, lamb, and other dishes.*

Makes about 1 cup

The Bailey Mint Sauce

½ cup distilled white vinegar
⅓ cup finely chopped mint leaves
2 tablespoons sugar
Green food coloring

In a nonaluminum saucepan, over medium heat, heat vinegar until warm. Add mint leaves and sugar, stirring until sugar is all dissolved. Add a few drops of green food color to add to the feeling!

Makes about ¾ cup

Bailey Family Fish Fry Lemon-Butter Sauce

½ cup butter or margarine
2 tablespoons lemon juice
1 tablespoon chopped parsley
1 pinch of garlic powder

In a saucepan, over medium heat, melt butter. Add lemon juice, parsley, and garlic powder. Heat to desired temperature, stirring constantly. *This is perfect for all types of seafood and on chicken dishes.*

Makes about ½ cup

Q: What did Mary do during World War II?

I'm Banking on Carter's Tartar Sauce

1 cup mayonnaise
1½ teaspoons grated onion
1 tablespoon minced dill pickle
1 teaspoon chopped parsley
1 teaspoon chopped pimiento
1 tablespoon dill pickle juice (from jar)
1 teaspoon sugar

In a mixing bowl, combine all ingredients and mix well. *Great with all types of seafoods, and on ham sandwiches. Can be stored in refrigerator for 5 days in a tightly covered container.*

Makes about 1¼ cups

***A:** She ran the USO.*

Breads and Muffins

"Donna knew that Frank Capra was a true artisan when it came to character development and film-making, in general. Although she had studied acting, she was eager to learn everything she could from Capra."

—*Grover Asmus* (Donna Reed's widower)

A delirious Uncle Billy (Thomas Mitchell) is confronted by George about the missing $8,000.

Old Man Gower (H. B. Warner) donates to the Baileys' cause.

Grandma Bailey's Old-Fashioned Buttermilk Biscuits

2 cups self-rising flour
1 cup buttermilk
¼ cup vegetable oil

Preheat oven to 450 degrees F. In a large mixing bowl, combine flour, oil, and buttermilk. Mix until dough easily comes away from side of bowl. Place dough on a floured bread sheet or wax paper. Roll dough with rolling pin or large glass, until ½ inch thick. Use top of glass to cut out biscuits. Place an inch apart in a lightly greased baking pan. Bake in preheated oven until golden brown, about 10 to 12 minutes. *These are great with butter, honey, jelly, eggs, or your favorite garnish. Also great for sopping up gravy.*

Makes 12 to 14 biscuits

Biscuit Sticks to Build On

2 cups all-purpose flour
½ teaspoon salt
3 teaspoons baking powder
¼ cup solid vegetable shortening
¾ cup milk

Preheat oven to 450 degrees F. In a large mixing bowl, sift flour, salt, and baking powder together. Cut in shortening with a pastry blender until well mixed. Stir in milk and make a soft dough. Place on a floured bread sheet or wax paper and roll until ¾ inch thick. Cut sticks 8 inches long with a knife. Place an inch apart in a lightly greased baking pan. Bake in preheated oven until golden brown, about 10 minutes.

Makes 14 to 16 biscuits

Bailey Irish Potato Biscuits

6 medium potatoes, unpeeled
1 tablespoon salt
8 tablespoons shortening
1¼ cups all-purpose flour

In a medium saucepan, cook potatoes in water, in skins, for 25 minutes. Remove from water and peel immediately.

Preheat oven to 375 degrees F. Place in a large bowl and mash lightly, leaving lumps. Add salt and shortening and mix lightly. Add flour and mix well. Form into a ball and roll out on a lightly floured bread sheet until 1 inch thick. Use top of glass to cut out biscuits. Place an inch apart on ungreased cookie sheet and prick with fork. Bake in preheated oven for about 1 hour, or until golden brown. Can be served warm or cold.

Makes about 14 to 16 biscuits

Bailey Park Old World Biscuits

1 pound all-purpose flour
½ tablespoon salt
1 teaspoon baking powder
½ pound solid vegetable shortening
1 pint sour cream
1 egg
1 egg yolk (optional)

Preheat oven to 350 degrees F. Sift flour, salt, and baking powder into a large bowl. Add shortening, sour cream, and egg; mix well with mixer. Place mixture on a lightly floured bread sheet and roll until 1 inch thick. Cut biscuits with top of glass. Place an inch apart on a greased cookie sheet and prick tops. (If desired, brush tops with beaten egg yolk.) Bake in preheated oven for 20 minutes, or until golden brown.

Makes 14 to 16 biscuits

***A:** She was a librarian.*

Silver Dollar Potter Pancakes

2 eggs, separated
2 tablespoons sugar
½ teaspoon salt
½ teaspoon baking soda
1 cup sour cream
1 cup sifted all-purpose flour

In a large mixing bowl, beat egg yolks and blend in sugar, salt, baking soda, and sour cream. Add all flour and mix until smooth. Beat egg whites until stiff. Fold whites into flour mixture. Drop by tablespoons onto hot, lightly greased griddle. Turn when one side bubbles. *Great with butter and syrup, jams, or your favorite topping.*

Makes 18 to 20 silver-dollar-size pancakes

Laura Bailey's Buttermilk Pancakes

2 eggs, beaten
2 tablespoons sugar
1 teaspoon salt
2½ cups buttermilk
2 cups all-purpose flour
1 teaspoon baking powder
1 teaspoon baking soda
¼ cup hot water
2 tablespoons butter or margarine, melted

In a large mixing bowl, combine beaten eggs, sugar, salt, and buttermilk. Sift flour and baking powder together; blend into egg mixture. Dissolve baking soda in hot water; stir into mixture. Add melted butter to mixture. Bake on a hot, greased griddle until golden brown on both sides.

About 20 pancakes

Q: What was the name of Uncle Billy's deceased wife?

Annie's Pancakes and Then Some

Pancakes are better when served with applesauce, fresh fruit, or with sour cream on top. It's also fun to create your own favorites!

1 egg
1 cup self-rising flour
3/4 cup milk
2 tablespoons vegetable oil
1 tablespoon sugar

In a large mixing bowl, beat egg until fluffy. Add all other ingredients and beat until smooth. Cook pancakes of desired size on hot, greased griddle until bubbly and dry around edges. Flip and cook until golden brown.

About 10 pancakes

BLUEBERRY PANCAKES
Stir in 3/4 cup fresh or thawed frozen blueberries.

WHOLE WHEAT PANCAKES
Substitute whole wheat flour for self-rising flour, and add 3 teaspoons baking powder and 1/2 teaspoon salt to mixture. Also substitute brown sugar for granulated sugar.

BANANA PANCAKES
Cut 1 large banana into small pieces and add to mixture.

Bert the Cop's Fill-'Em-Up-and-Go Doughnuts

3 1/4 cups self-rising flour
1 cup sugar
1/2 teaspoon cinnamon
2 tablespoons vegetable shortening
2 eggs
3/4 cup milk
Vegetable oil

***A:** His late wife was named Laura.*

Beat 1½ cups flour and all remaining ingredients except oil in a large mixing bowl at low speed for about 30 seconds, constantly scraping bowl. Now beat on medium speed for 2 minutes. Stir in remaining flour and turn dough onto well-floured bread sheet. Lightly coat dough with flour and gently roll until about ⅜ inch thick. Cut with doughnut cutter, flouring cutter between cuts. Heat 3 inches vegetable oil in a deep fryer or large kettle to 375 F. Gently slide doughnuts into hot oil with wide spatula. Turn doughnuts over when they rise to the top. Remove when golden brown. Drain on paper towels. *For a tasty treat, gently shake doughnuts one at a time in bags of powdered sugar, granulated sugar with cinnamon, or drizzle melted chocolate on top.*

Makes 24 servings

Ernie Bishop's Down-Home Crullers

2½ cups all-purpose flour
½ cup sour cream
6 egg yolks
1 teaspoon salt
2 tablespoons sugar
1 tablespoon brandy
Vegetable oil

In a large bowl, combine flour, egg yolks, and sour cream to make a soft dough. Add salt, sugar, and brandy. Knead until smooth. Place on a lightly floured bread sheet and roll until very thin, about ⅛ inch thick. Cut into diamond shapes. Cut a slit in the center and pull one end through. Heat 2 inches vegetable oil in a deep fryer or large kettle to 375 degrees F. Fry 4 to 6 at a time until light brown, about 30 seconds, and drain on paper towels. *Sprinkle with cinnamon or confectioners' sugar, or dip plain in honey.*

About 2 dozen crullers

Q: How old was Uncle Billy when Peter Bailey died?

Uncle Billy's Pet Hush Puppies

2⅓ cups yellow cornmeal
1 teaspoon salt
2½ tablespoons green onion, with tops, chopped fine
1 medium carrot, grated
¾ teaspoon baking soda
1½ cups buttermilk

In a large bowl, mix cornmeal, salt, green onion, carrot, and baking soda. Stir in buttermilk. Heat 1 inch of vegetable oil in a deep fryer or kettle to 375 degrees F. Drop by spoonfuls into hot oil. Fry until golden brown and drain on paper towels.

About 24 hush puppies

Violet's Always Sweet Blueberry Muffins

2 cups all-purpose flour
¼ teaspoon salt
4 teaspoons baking powder
3 tablespoons sugar
1 egg, beaten
1 cup milk
2 tablespoons butter or margarine, melted
1¼ cups fresh blueberries, or thawed frozen blueberries

Preheat oven to 350 degrees F. In a mixing bowl, sift all dry ingredients together. In another bowl, combine egg, milk, and melted butter, and then combine with dry ingredients. Fold blueberries into batter. Fill well-greased muffin tins a third full with mixture. Bake in preheated oven for 25 minutes.

About 12 muffins

***A:** He was fifty-six.*

Charleston Twirl Cinnamon Rolls

1 package active dry yeast
1/4 cup warm water
1 3/4 cups scalded milk
1/2 cup butter or margarine
3/4 cup sugar
1 teaspoon salt
1 egg
5 1/2 to 6 cups all-purpose flour
1/2 cup butter or margarine, melted
3 tablespoons sugar
Cinnamon to taste

In a bowl, dissolve yeast in warm water. In another bowl, combine scalded milk, ½ cup butter, ¾ cup sugar, and salt; set aside. When lukewarm, add egg, yeast, and flour. (You may not need all 6 cups to make a kneadable dough.) Knead dough on lightly floured bread sheet until smooth. Cover and let rise in a warm place until double in size. Roll on lightly floured bread sheet until 1/4 inch thick. Brush with melted butter and sprinkle sugar and cinnamon to taste. Roll and cut into 1-inch pieces. Cover and let rise in a warm place until double in size.

Preheat oven to 350 degrees F. Place rolls an inch apart in a greased, shallow pan and sprinkle tops with sugar and cinnamon. Bake in preheated oven for 25 minutes.

About 36 rolls

Pizza Crust Alla Mr. Martini

1 tablespoon active dry yeast
2 teaspoons salt
4 tablespoons sugar
2 cups warm water
1/4 cup olive oil
2 cups semolina flour
3 cups all-purpose flour

Q: What was Uncle Billy's telephone number?

In a large mixing bowl, combine yeast, salt, and sugar. Add warm water and olive oil and stir well. Add semolina flour and all-purpose flour. (Add more flour, pinch by pinch, if needed to make dough not sticky.) Knead dough until soft. *This is a basic pizza crust. See Entrees for pizza recipe.*

Makes two 12-inch pizza crusts.

Sam Wainwright's Rolling-in-the-Dough Bread

1 package active dry yeast
¼ cup warm water
2 cups milk
2 tablespoons sugar
1 tablespoon vegetable shortening
2 teaspoons salt
6 cups all-purpose flour
¼ cup butter, melted

In a small bowl, dissolve yeast in warm water. In a small saucepan, combine milk, sugar, shortening, and salt, and heat over medium heat until warm; stirring constantly. Put in a large mixing bowl and combine with 2 cups flour; beat well. Add the yeast and stir until smooth. Stir in as much remaining flour as you can mix with a spoon. Turn out onto lightly floured bread sheet and stir in any remaining flour. Knead dough until stiff and smooth. Shape into a ball and place in a lightly greased bowl, turning once to grease surface. Cover and let rise in a warm place until double in size.

Turn onto lightly floured bread sheet and cut in half. Shape into 2 balls; cover and let rest 10 minutes. While waiting, grease two 8×4-inch bread pans. Shape balls into loaves and place in pans. Brush with melted butter. Cover and let rise in warm spot for 60 minutes.

Preheat oven to 375 degrees F. Bake in preheated oven for about 40 to 45 minutes, or until bread makes a hollow sound when tapped. Remove from pans and let cool on wire racks.

Makes 2 loaves

A:* BE*dford-247.

Hee-Haw Corn Bread

1½ cups cornmeal
½ cup self-rising flour
1 teaspoon baking powder
1 teaspoon sugar
½ teaspoon baking soda
⅓ cup vegetable shortening
1½ cups buttermilk
2 eggs

Preheat oven to 450 degrees F. In a large mixing bowl, mix all ingredients by beating vigorously for 30 seconds. Pour into a well-greased 9-inch round cake pan. Bake in preheated oven until golden brown, 25 to 30 minutes. *Great with chili, stews, eggs, sauces.*

8 to 10 servings

Mary Bailey's After-School Healthy Bread Treat

1 cup wheat bran
¼ cup dark brown sugar
2½ cups fresh pear/peach/pineapple mixture
½ cup wheat germ
½ cup natural applesauce
1 cup 2 percent milk
½ cup orange juice
1½ cups all-purpose flour

Preheat oven to 350 degrees F. In a large mixing bowl, combine bran, brown sugar, fruit, wheat germ, applesauce, and milk. Blend with a spoon and let stand for 25 minutes. Add orange juice and flour; mix thoroughly. Place in a 9×5×3-inch bread pan. Bake in pre-heated oven for 45 to 50 minutes, until lightly brown. Let cool and slice.

Makes 1 loaf

Q: What year did Harry Bailey graduate from high school?

"I Must Be Off My Nut" Banana Bread

¼ cup vegetable shortening
½ cup sugar
1 egg
1 cup wheat bran
1½ cups mashed bananas (2 large bananas)
1 teaspoon vanilla extract
1½ cups all-purpose flour, sifted
2 teaspoons baking powder
½ teaspoon baking soda
½ teaspoon salt
½ cup walnuts, chopped

Preheat oven to 350 degrees F. In a large mixing bowl, blend shortening and sugar thoroughly. Add egg and beat well. Stir in bran, bananas, and vanilla. In another bowl, sift together flour, baking powder, baking soda, and salt. Add to banana mixture along with nuts, stirring until well combined. Turn into a 9×5×3-inch bread pan and bake in preheated oven for about 1 hour, or until a toothpick inserted in middle comes out clean.

Makes 1 loaf

Parlez-Vous Français French Toast

8–10 slices white or whole wheat bread, cut in halves
2 eggs
½ cup milk
Butter or margarine, as needed
Cinnamon
Confectioners' sugar
Syrup or honey

***A:** He graduated in 1928 from Bedford Falls High School.*

In a medium mixing bowl, beat eggs. Add milk and mix well. Melt butter in a large skillet over medium heat. Dip bread slices in egg mixture and fry until golden brown on bottom. Turn once and fry the other side. Sprinkle cinnamon and confectioners' sugar on top. Serve with syrup or honey.

8 to 10 servings

Sunday Come-to-Dinner Rolls

1 cup milk
½ cup butter or margarine
½ cup sugar
1 teaspoon salt
1 package active dry yeast
¼ cup water, at room temperature
3 eggs
4½ cups all-purpose flour

In a small saucepan, scald milk. In a large mixing bowl, combine milk, butter, sugar, and salt; let cool. In a separate bowl, dissolve yeast in ¼ cup lukewarm water. Add yeast and eggs to milk mixture and beat well. Stir in all flour until dough is sticky. Cover and let rise in warm place until doubled in size, about 1½ to 2 hours.

Punch down dough, and shape into 1-inch balls. Place three balls each in lightly greased muffin tins; let stand until doubled in size, about 20 minutes.

Preheat oven to 400 degrees F. and bake for 16 to 18 minutes.

About 30 rolls

George gives a piece of his mind to Old Man Potter (Lionel Barrymore) and his bodyguard (Frank Hagney).

Salads

"This film is so special to so many people, not just here but in different parts of the world as well. I'm amazed at all the stories I've heard over the years about how the film has affected people. I'm truly glad to have been a part of it."

—*Jimmy Stewart* (George Bailey)

George is despondent, fearing that the missing $8,000 will ruin his business and his family.

Mary gives George their honeymoon money to stop the Bailey Building & Loan from closing.

Lights-Out Cucumber Salad

2 large cucumbers
1 medium onion
3/4 cup sour cream
1/4 cup distilled white vinegar
1/2 teaspoon salt
1/4 teaspoon pepper
1 teaspoon sugar

Wash cucumbers and dice into bite-size cubes. Place in a large serving bowl. Slice onion crosswise and separate into rings; add to cucumbers. In a small bowl, mix sour cream, vinegar, salt, pepper, and sugar, and pour over cucumbers, mixing well. Can be eaten at once or chilled.

4 to 6 servings

Capra Corn Salad

1 (16-ounce) bag of frozen corn
1/8 head cabbage
1 small sweet red bell pepper
2 stalks celery
1/4 cup distilled white vinegar
Salt and pepper to taste
1/4 cup water
1 teaspoon prepared mustard

Cook corn in water according to directions on bag, drain, and set aside. Chop cabbage, red pepper, and celery. Place in a medium saucepan, cover with water, and boil together, covered for 10 minutes. Drain vegetables. Mix corn, vegetables, vinegar, salt and pepper, water, and mustard; mix well. Serve chilled.

6 servings

Q: What sport did Harry play at college?

Mrs. Hatch's Fruit Salad Surprise

1 (6-ounce) package lime-flavored gelatin
1 cup hot water
1 cup half-and-half
1 (16-ounce) can fruit cocktail, drained
1 cup large-curd cottage cheese
½ cup chopped pecans
½ cup mayonnaise

Dissolve gelatin in hot water and cool slightly. Stir in half-and-half, and cool until partially set, stirring frequently to maintain smoothness. Fold in remaining ingredients. Pour into 9×9-inch pan, cover, and chill until firm. Cut into square serving-size pieces. Serve by itself or on crisp lettuce leaves.

6 to 8 servings

"He Melts When He Sees-Her" Salad

1 hard-boiled egg
1 garlic clove, cut in half
⅓ cup olive oil
1 teaspoon Worcestershire sauce
¼ teaspoon dry mustard
Salt and pepper to taste
1 large head romaine lettuce, cut or torn into bite-size bits
1 tablespoon lemon juice
1 cup croutons
⅓ cup grated Parmesan cheese

Peel hard-boiled egg and set aside. Rub large serving bowl (preferably wooden) with one garlic half. Finely chop remaining garlic and put in bowl. In a mixing bowl, mix oil, Worcestershire, mustard, salt, and pepper. Put romaine in serving bowl and add dressing; toss until leaves glisten. Chop egg and sprinkle over salad. Pour lemon juice on salad; toss well. Add croutons and cheese to top of salad; serve.

4 to 6 servings

***A:** Harry played football and made second string All-American.*

Hero's Welcome Garden Salad

1 head iceberg lettuce
1 red onion
½ small green bell pepper
2 stalks celery
½ small cucumber
4 radishes
2 medium carrots
¼ cup shredded Cheddar cheese (optional)
1 hard-boiled egg (optional)

Cut or tear lettuce into bite-size pieces and place in large serving bowl. Cut all other vegetables into small pieces and add to lettuce; toss well. If you wish, sprinkle cheese on top and garnish with egg slices. *Serve with your favorite dressing.*

6 to 8 servings

George's Lust for Adventure Mandarin Salad

⅓ cup sliced almonds
2 teaspoons sugar
¼ head iceberg lettuce, cut into bite-size pieces
¼ head romaine lettuce, cut into bite-size pieces
2 green onions, sliced thin
1 cup chopped celery
Ready-made sweet-and-sour dressing to taste
1 (12-ounce) can mandarin orange segments, drained

In a small skillet, over low heat, cook almonds and sugar, stirring constantly, until all the sugar is melted and almonds are coated. Let cool and break apart. Place lettuce and romaine in a large plastic storage bag; add onions and celery. Pour sweet-and-sour dressing into bag; add orange segments. Seal bag tightly and shake well until salad greens and orange segments are thoroughly coated. Add almonds; shake and serve in a large bowl.

4 servings

Q: What was Harry's wife's name?

Macaroni alla Martini

1 (12-ounce) box elbow macaroni
2 stalks celery
1 carrot, chopped fine
1 small onion, chopped fine
1 teaspoon sugar
3/4–1 cup mayonnaise or salad dressing
Salt and pepper to taste

Prepare macaroni according to instructions on box; drain and place in a serving bowl. Add celery, carrot, onion, and sugar, and stir in mayonnaise. (Start with 3/4 cup and add more by teaspoons to desired consistency.) Salt and pepper to taste. *Great on lettuce with whole wheat crackers.*

6 servings

Cousin Eustace Eggs-actly on the Money Salad

8 eggs
2 stalks celery, diced
1 small onion, chopped fine
Salt and pepper to taste
3 heaping tablespoons mayonnaise (or more)

Place all eggs in medium saucepan; cover with cold water. Bring to a boil, reduce heat, and cook 8 minutes. Remove pan from heat and run cold water into it until eggs feel cool to the touch. Crack and peel eggs. Chop into bite-size pieces and place in a large mixing bowl. Add celery, onion, salt and pepper, and 3 heaping tablespoons mayonnaise. (More mayonnaise may be added if desired.) Blend well. *Serve on bed of lettuce with wheat crackers, or on favorite bread as a sandwich.*

4 servings

***A:** Ruth Dakin-Bailey.*

Victory Garden Potato Salad

This recipe is for a good-size picnic. It can be halved for regular family meals.

12 medium potatoes (unpeeled)
10 eggs
2 large onions, chopped fine
8 radishes, chopped fine
4 stalks celery, sliced thin
2 medium-sweet pickles, chopped fine
2 cups mayonnaise or Miracle Whip (or more)
½ cup slaw dressing (Marzetti's is great)
3 tablespoons prepared yellow mustard
Salt and pepper to taste
Dash of paprika

Boil potatoes until tender; let stand until cool enough to handle comfortably. Place eggs in medium saucepan and cover with cold water. Bring eggs to a boil; reduce heat and cook for 8 minutes. Remove from heat and run cold water in pan until eggs are well cooled. Peel potatoes and cut into bite-size pieces. (Skins may be left on for added flavor.) Put potatoes in a large serving dish. Crack and peel 8 eggs; coarsely chop and add to potatoes. Add onions, radishes, celery, and pickles; mix gently. Add two cups mayonnaise, slaw dressing, and mustard; mix well. Add more mayonnaise, by the tablespoon, if desired. Salt and pepper to taste.

Peel remaining 2 eggs, cut into medium-thick slices, and arrange on top of salad. Sprinkle with paprika for added color. Chill and serve.

12 to 14 servings

Q: What kind of job did her father give Harry?

320 Sycamore Waldorf Salad

2 medium apples, cored and diced
2 stalks celery, chopped
½ cup chopped walnuts
½ cup mayonnaise or salad dressing
Lettuce cups

Toss apples, celery and walnuts with mayonnaise. Spoon into lettuce cups. *This mixture can also be tossed with shredded lettuce and served in salad bowls.*

6 servings

Shell-Shocked Chicken Salad

By all means substitute home-cooked chicken breast cubes if available.

1 teaspoon olive or corn oil
1 (12-ounce) package macaroni shells or spirals
1 (10-ounce) can chicken breast in spring water, drained and separated into bite-size pieces
2 stalks celery, diced
1 small onion, chopped fine
4–5 heaping tablespoons of mayonnaise (or more)
Salt and pepper to taste

In a large saucepan, bring 8 cups water to a boil. Add oil and macaroni; cook until tender, according to package directions. Remove from heat and drain. In a large mixing bowl or serving dish, combine macaroni, chicken, celery, onion, 4 to 5 heaping tablespoons mayonnaise, and salt and pepper. (More mayonnaise may be added if desired.) *Serve on a bed of lettuce with wheat crackers or pita bread.*

4 to 6 servings

A: *Research in his glass factory.*

J. W. Hatched Chicken Salad

1 (10-ounce) can breast of chicken, drained and separated into bite-size pieces (or use fresh-cooked chicken cubes)
2 celery stalks, diced
1 small onion, chopped fine
3 heaping tablespoons mayonnaise or tangy salad dressing
Salt and pepper to taste

In a large mixing bowl, mix chicken, celery, onion, and mayonnaise. Salt and pepper to taste. *Serve on a bed of lettuce with wheat crackers or on favorite bread as a sandwich.*

4 servings

Creamy Crabby Potter Pasta Salad

1 egg white
1 teaspoon Dijon-style mustard
1 teaspoon lemon or lime juice
Salt and pepper to taste
1/8 teaspoon garlic powder
2 1/2 tablespoons plain nonfat yogurt
1 1/3 cups uncooked rotini pasta
1/2 cup broccoli florets
1/2 cup cauliflower florets
1/3 cup diced carrots
1 cup imitation crab legs, chopped
1/2 cup Swiss cheese, cut into bite-size pieces
1 large green onion, with top, sliced

In a blender cup, combine egg white, Dijon mustard, lemon juice, salt and pepper, garlic powder, and yogurt. Blend at high speed for 25 to 30 seconds; set aside. In a medium saucepan, cook pasta according to package directions, until tender; drain and let cool. In a large mixing bowl, combine pasta, broccoli, cauliflower, carrots, crab legs, Swiss cheese, and green onion. Pour in yogurt mixture and mix gently. Cover and chill.

4 to 6 servings

Q: How many planes did Harry shoot down in a World War II battle and what medal did he win?

Mount Bedford Wild Raspberry Salad

2 (4-ounce) packages raspberry-flavored gelatin
2 cups boiling water
1 (16-ounce) jar applesauce
2 (10-ounce) boxes frozen raspberries, thawed
1 cup mini marshmallows
Whipped cream

Pour the gelatin in water, stirring until completely dissolved. Add applesauce, undrained raspberries, and mini marshmallows; mix well. Pour into a 9×13-inch serving dish and chill until set. Cut into cubes; serve with dollop of whipped cream on top.

12 servings

Rainy-Day Wedding Wild Rice Salad

1 cup cooked wild rice
1 cup imitation crab legs, chopped
1 cup frozen peas, thawed
½ cup diced green bell pepper
½ cup diced sweet red bell pepper
4 green onions, with green tops, chopped
1 (6-ounce) can sliced water chestnuts, well drained
1 cup sliced celery
1 cup mayonnaise
2 tablespoons lemon juice
Salt and pepper to taste

Combine the wild rice, crab meat, and vegetables in a large mixing or serving bowl. In a small bowl, combine mayonnaise, lemon juice, salt, and pepper. Pour dressing over salad; toss well. Can be served warm or slightly chilled.

4 to 6 servings

***A:** Fifteen planes, including two that were headed for a loaded transport, and he won the Congressional Medal of Honor.*

Mama Dollar and Papa Dollar Spinach Salad

8 ounces fresh spinach, washed and stemmed
4 small tomatoes, quartered
1 cup shredded mozzarella cheese
1 small red onion, sliced very thin and separated into rings
2 garlic cloves, chopped fine
1 teaspoon oregano
1 cup Italian dressing

Combine all ingredients in a large mixing or serving bowl and toss until all is moist.

4 servings

Colors of Christmas Cauliflower Salad

1 head cauliflower
1 cup radishes, sliced thin
½ cup sliced green onions, with green tops
1 (8-ounce) can sliced water chestnuts, well drained
¾ cup sour cream
¾ cup mayonnaise
1 small package buttermilk salad dressing mix

Cut cauliflower into bite-size pieces, wash, and drain well. In a large serving bowl, combine cauliflower, radishes, green onions, and water chestnuts; toss gently. In a medium bowl, mix remaining ingredients; pour over vegetables. Mix until completely covered. Best if served chilled.

6 to 8 servings

Q: What was Sam Wainwright's favorite phrase?

Seventh Heaven Layer Salad

6–7 cups iceberg lettuce, torn into bite-size pieces
½ cup sliced green onions, with green tops
Salt and pepper to taste
Sugar to taste
6 hard-boiled eggs, sliced
½ cup chopped walnuts
1 (10-ounce) package frozen peas, thawed
1 pound bacon slices, cooked and crumbled
1 ½ cups shredded Swiss cheese
1 ½ cups mayonnaise
½ cup shredded Cheddar cheese

Line bottom of large salad or serving bowl with 3 cups lettuce. Add green onions in a layer; salt, pepper, and sugar to taste. Add eggs in a layer; salt to taste. In separate layers, add walnuts, peas, remaining 3 to 4 cups lettuce, bacon, and Swiss cheese. Cover completely with mayonnaise and refrigerate for 24 hours. Sprinkle with Cheddar cheese and serve.

8 to 10 servings

Under-the-Bridge Tuna Salad

1 (10-ounce) can of tuna in spring water, well drained
2 celery stalks, diced
1 small onion, chopped fine
3 heaping tablespoons mayonnaise or tangy salad dressing
Salt and pepper to taste

In a large mixing bowl, mix tuna, celery, onion, and mayonnaise. Salt and pepper to taste. *Serve on a bed of lettuce with wheat crackers or on favorite bread as a sandwich.*

4 servings

A: *"Hee-haw."*

Cauli-Broc Salad

This delicious recipe is from Carol Coombs Mueller, who played Janie Bailey.

1 head cauliflower
2 heads broccoli
1 small onion, sliced thin
1 (2-ounce) jar pimientos, chopped
½ green bell pepper, chopped
½ sweet red pepper, chopped
1 cup mayonnaise
⅓ cup distilled white vinegar
⅓ cup sugar
Salt and pepper to taste

Cut or break cauliflower and broccoli into bite size-pieces. Combine cauliflower, broccoli, onion, pimiento, and peppers in a large serving bowl; toss well. In a small bowl combine mayonnaise, vinegar, sugar, salt, and pepper; mix well. Pour over vegetables. *Best if allowed to sit overnight.*

10 to 12 servings

Luncheon Fruit Salad

Another tasty salad recipe from Carol Coombs Mueller.

1 (16-ounce) container small-curd cottage cheese
1 (3-ounce) package orange-flavored gelatin
1 (11-ounce) can mandarin oranges, well drained
1 cup whipped cream

Dissolve orange gelatin according to package instructions. In a medium serving dish, combine gelatin, cottage cheese, mandarin oranges, and whipped cream. Chill and serve. *Better if served the next day.*

4 to 6 servings

Q: What did Sam invest in and develop?

Mrs. Hatch's Cheesy Corn Bread Salad

1 (7-ounce) box corn muffin mix
1 tomato, chopped
8 green onions, with green tops, chopped
1 (15-ounce) can corn, drained
1 (14-ounce) can pinto beans, drained
2 cups grated Cheddar cheese
10 slices bacon, cooked crisp and crumbled
1 package ranch salad dressing mix

Prepare corn muffin mix according to package directions. Crumble corn bread when cool. Place half the corn bread in a large serving bowl. In a separate bowl mix tomatoes and onions. Over corn bread, layer half the corn, half the beans, half the tomato mixture, and half the cheese. Sprinkle half the bacon on mixture and top with half the of dressing. Repeat layers. *Best if allowed to sit for a while.*

6 to 8 servings

Bailey Park Picnic Coleslaw

1 small head cabbage, shredded or finely chopped
4 medium carrots, washed and shredded
½ small onion, chopped fine
¼ cup sour cream
¼ cup mayonnaise (about: amount can vary with desired consistency)
3 tablespoons slaw dressing (about), Marzetti's is best
Salt and pepper to taste
1 teaspoon sugar
Paprika

In a large mixing bowl, combine shredded cabbage, carrots, and onion. In a separate bowl, mix together all other ingredients except paprika. Spoon dressing into cabbage mixture and mix well. Add more mayonnaise or slaw dressing to suit your taste. Sprinkle top with paprika before serving.

10 to 12 servings

***A:** Plastics, made from soybeans.*

Entrees

"Beulah [Bondi] *was particularly interested in the fact that all the details were so carefully planned, including objects on the back of the upholstered chairs and sofa that looked to me like lace doilies. She said the doilies were called antimacassars. Macassar oil, it seems, was a rather pungent preparation that men were accustomed to wearing on their hair, and the antimacassar was placed to keep the oil off the upholstery. Quite an important fact, I guess, in antique lore."*

—*Virginia Patton Moss* (Ruth Dakin Bailey)

Peter Bailey needs help spelling for his holiday play.

Mount Bedford Roast Beef

4 pound rolled beef rump
2 tablespoons salt
2 teaspoons pepper
3 tablespoons butter or margarine
Mrs. Dash seasoning (optional)
1¼ cups water
2 garlic cloves, minced
1 bay leaf
9 small potatoes, peeled
10 medium carrots, peeled
8 small onions

Preheat oven to 350 degrees F. Set roast on cutting board and sprinkle with 1 tablespoon salt and 1 teaspoon pepper. In a large dutch oven, over medium heat, melt butter and brown roast on all sides. Sprinkle remaining salt and pepper on roast. (A few sprinkles of Mrs. Dash or other seasoning is also good!) Add water and bring to a boil. Remove from heat and place roast and all juices, garlic, and bay leaf in a roasting pan. Cook in preheated oven for 2½ hours, basting occasionally. Add all vegetables and a pinch of seasonings. Cook until vegetables are tender, approximately 1 hour.

For excellent gravy, remove roast and vegetables from pan and skim off as much grease as possible from liquid. Add enough water to liquid remaining in pan to make 2 cups. Shake ½ cup water and 2 tablespoons all-purpose flour together in a sealed container and gradually add to liquid. Heat to boiling in a small saucepan, stirring constantly. *Great over meat and vegetables.*

8 servings

Q: Sam Wainwright came to visit George and Mary while on his way to what state?

"Buffalo Gals, Won't You Come Out Tonight" Beef Stew

1 pound stewing beef, cut into bite-size pieces
2 tablespoons butter or margarine
4 cups water
Salt and pepper to taste
2 garlic cloves, minced
1 tablespoon ketchup
½ tablespoon prepared yellow mustard
1 beef bouillon cube
Mrs. Dash seasoning (optional)
1 (16-ounce) package mixed vegetables
3 large potatoes, peeled and cubed
3 stalks celery, sliced
2 medium onions, cubed
1 tomato, cubed
1 tablespoon cornstarch

In a large dutch oven, over medium heat, brown meat in butter on all sides. Add water, salt and pepper, garlic, ketchup, mustard, and bouillon cube. (A pinch or two of Mrs. Dash is optional.) Bring to a boil. Reduce heat and simmer, covered, for 1½ hours. Stir occasionally and add small amounts of water if necessary. Add all vegetables, enough water to cover, and bring to a rapid boil. Reduce heat and simmer, covered, for 1 hour, or until vegetables are tender. A pinch more seasonings may be added. 15 minutes before serving, add cornstarch to ½ cup water and shake in a tightly closed container. Gradually stir into stew. Cook until gravy is slightly thickened.

6 servings

***A:** Florida.*

Buffalo Gals Beef Stroganoff

1 pound stewing beef, cut into bite-size pieces
2 tablespoons butter or margarine
2 cups water
1 beef bouillon cube
2 tablespoons ketchup
½ tablespoon prepared yellow mustard
1 garlic clove, minced
Salt and pepper to taste
1 (8-ounce) can sliced mushrooms, drained
1 medium onion, chopped fine
3 tablespoons flour
½ cup water
1 cup sour cream
Cooked noodles, as desired

In a large dutch oven, over medium heat, brown meat in butter on all sides. Add water, bouillon cube, ketchup, mustard, garlic, and salt and pepper. Bring to a boil. Reduce heat and simmer, covered, for 1 to 1½ hours, stirring occasionally. (More water may be added if necessary.) Add mushrooms and onion and simmer for 10 minutes. Shake flour and water in a tightly closed container; stir gradually into beef mixture. Bring to a boil, stirring constantly until thicker. Stir in sour cream and stir until hot and creamy. Serve over cooked noodles.

4 servings

Q: What was Sam's wife's name?

Roast Potter and Noodles

3 pounds beef arm roast or chuck eye roast
Salt and pepper to taste
Flour
3 tablespoons butter or margarine
2 small onions, chopped
1 garlic clove, chopped
1 (10¾-ounce) can condensed cream of mushroom soup
2 soup cans water
Cooked noodles, as desired

On a cutting board, season roast with salt and pepper. Sprinkle whole roast with flour. In a large dutch oven, over medium heat, brown roast in butter. Add onions, garlic, soup, and water. Bring to a boil. Reduce heat and simmer, covered, for about 3 hours, stirring and basting occasionally, until tender (make a small knife cut to check doneness). Slice meat thin and serve over noodles. *Sauce from pan is a tasty addition to the meat and noodles.*

6 servings

Mr. Welch's In a Stew Beefy Feast

2½ pounds stewing beef
Salt and pepper to taste
1 (8-ounce) can mushrooms, drained, juice reserved
2 tablespoons steak sauce
1 garlic clove, minced
1 (1-ounce) package dry onion soup mix

Preheat oven to 350 degrees F. On a cutting board, season beef with salt and pepper. In a mixing bowl, mix mushroom juice, steak sauce, garlic, and soup mix. Pour half the sauce into a large casserole dish. Place meat in dish and cover with mushrooms. Add remaining sauce and a pinch of pepper. Cover and cook in preheated oven for 1½ hours, or until tender, basting occasionally.

4 to 6 servings

***A:** Jane.*

A-Taskit, A-Tisket, It's Annie's Home-Style Brisket

2½-pound boneless beef brisket, well trimmed
Salt and pepper to taste
1 medium onion, chopped fine
1 garlic clove, minced
¼ cup barbecue sauce
¼ cup ketchup
¼ cup distilled white vinegar
1 tablespoon Worcestershire sauce
1 tablespoon steak sauce
¼ cup dark brown sugar

Preheat oven to 350 degrees F. On a cutting board, sprinkle whole brisket with salt and pepper. Place meat in a 9×14×2-inch baking pan. In a mixing bowl, mix remaining ingredients and pour over meat. Cover and cook in preheated oven for about 2 hours, or until tender. Slice thin and serve with sauce from pan. *Also makes a great sandwich.*

8 to 10 servings

Fifty-Cents-on-the-Dollar Chuck Roast

3-pound chuck roast
Salt and pepper to taste
1 (1-ounce) package onion soup mix
1 (10¾-ounce) can condensed cream of mushroom soup
½ soup can water
2 medium onions, quartered

Preheat oven to 325 degrees F. Season meat to taste. Place meat in a large casserole and cover with onion soup mix. Add mushroom soup, water, and onions. Cover and cook in pre-heated oven for about 3 hours. *Great with mashed potatoes, green beans, and biscuits.*

6 servings

Q: How much did Sam authorize to advance George when Uncle Billy lost the money?

Bedford Falls Blue Plate Special Meat Loaf

1 pound ground sirloin or ground round
1 egg, beaten
Salt and pepper to taste
Pinch of garlic powder
1 cup dried bread crumbs
1 cup croutons
1 cup milk
1 small onion, chopped fine
1 can cream of mushroom soup
1 (6-ounce) can tomato paste
2 tablespoons barbecue sauce

Preheat the oven to 350 degrees F. In a large mixing bowl, combine all ingredients except tomato paste and barbecue sauce. Place mixture in a greased suitable-sized casserole dish. Bake, covered, in preheated oven for 30 minutes. Mix tomato sauce and barbecue sauce. Remove cover and spread sauce on top of meat. Return to oven and bake, uncovered, an additional 15 to 25 minutes, or until sauce begins to glaze the meat.

4 to 6 servings

Bailey-Style Corned Beef and Cabbage

2 pounds well-trimmed corned beef, cut into eighths
1 small onion, cubed
1 garlic clove, minced
1 teaspoon salt
1 teaspoon pepper
1 small head cabbage, cut into eighths
1 large carrot, sliced

Place corned beef in a large dutch oven and add enough water to cover. Add onion, garlic, salt, and pepper. Bring to a boil over high heat; reduce heat and simmer, covered, for about 2 hours, or until beef is tender. Skim fat from top of cooking liquid. Remove beef. Add cabbage and carrot; bring to a boil. Reduce heat and simmer, uncovered, for 20 minutes. Return beef to liquid; heat until warmed through.

8 servings

A:* *$25,000.

Mr. Partridge's "Principal" Hamburger Casserole

1 pound ground sirloin
2 tablespoons butter or margarine
1 small onion, chopped fine
½ small green bell pepper, chopped
2 teaspoons chili powder
Salt and pepper to taste
1 cup raw rice
1 (20-ounce) can tomatoes
1 (5½-ounce) can tomato juice
Cooked noodles to suit

Preheat oven to 350 degrees F. In a large skillet, over medium heat, brown meat in butter. Add onion and green pepper and cook until vegetables are tender. Add remaining ingredients and stir well. Pour mixture into a large casserole and cook, covered, in preheated oven for 45 minutes. Serve over noodles.

4 servings

Bedford Falls High-School Cafeteria Goulash

1 pound ground chuck
1 medium onion, chopped fine
Salt and pepper to taste
1 garlic clove, minced
2 (15-ounce) cans stewed tomatoes
1 (12-ounce) package shell macaroni, cooked according to package instructions
1 (4-ounce) can mushrooms, drained and sliced
1 (8-ounce) can tomato sauce
1 teaspoon sugar

In a large skillet, over medium heat, brown meat; drain off fat. Add onion, seasonings, and garlic, and cook until tender. Add tomatoes, macaroni, mushrooms, tomato sauce, and sugar; stir. Simmer, uncovered, until less watery and hot.

6 to 8 servings

Q: What did young Violet Bick order at Gower's drug store?

Spinster Swiss Steak

1 pound top round steak
Salt and pepper to taste
Pinch of garlic powder
4 tablespoons flour
1 tablespoon butter or margarine
1 cup water
1 medium onion, sliced
1 garlic clove, minced
1 tablespoon ketchup
1 beef bouillon cube, dissolved in ½ cup water

Cut meat into quarters and season with salt, pepper, and garlic powder. Sprinkle 2 tablespoons of the flour on meat and pound in (both sides). In a large skillet, over medium to high heat, brown meat in butter. Add all other ingredients except remaining 2 tablespoons flour. Bring to a boil. Reduce heat and simmer, covered, for about 45 minutes, or until beef is tender. Remove meat from skillet. Mix remaining 2 tablespoons flour in ¼ cup water in a tightly closed container. Gradually stir flour mixture into liquid in skillet, until it reaches the consistency of gravy. Return meat to skillet and heat to desired temperature. *Gravy is great over meat and mashed potatoes.*

Serves 4

$20,000-a-Year Stuffed Pockets Cabbage Rolls

1 medium head cabbage, cored
1 medium onion, chopped fine
2 tablespoons butter or margarine
1 pound ground beef-pork mixture
Salt and pepper to taste
1 teaspoon paprika
½ cup raw rice
1 egg
1 garlic clove, minced
1 (16-ounce) can tomato sauce
1 (6-ounce) can tomato paste

***A:** Two cents worth of shoelaces (licorice).*

Preheat oven to 350 degrees F. Boil a good amount of water in a large pot. Place cabbage in boiling water and hold the head in place with a long fork. Cut away leaves as they begin to wilt, and remove them from the water; set aside. (You will need about 10 to 12 leaves.) In a skillet, over medium heat, sauté onion in melted butter until tender. In a large mixing bowl, combine meat, cooked onions, seasonings, rice, egg, and garlic. Take a good-sized handful of meat and place it in the center of a cabbage leaf. Spread the meat out slightly and roll up, tucking in sides. Place cabbage rolls in a large casserole dish. In a mixing bowl, blend tomato sauce with tomato paste; pour over cabbage rolls. Bake, covered, in preheated oven for about 1 hour, or until tender. *Tastes great with boiled potatoes and fresh bread.*

10 to 12 servings

Potter's Stuffed-Shirt Peppers

6 medium green bell peppers
1 pound ground beef-pork mixture
2 tablespoons butter or margarine
1 medium onion, chopped fine
¾ cup raw rice
Salt and pepper to taste
1 egg
1 (16-ounce) can tomato sauce
1 cup shredded mozzarella cheese

Preheat oven to 350 degrees F. Wash peppers and cut off tops, leaving about three quarters of the pepper. Remove all seeds and scrape out membranes with a spoon; set peppers aside. In a skillet, brown meat in butter. Add onion and cook until tender. Drain and place mixture in a large mixing bowl. Add rice, salt, pepper, and egg, mixing well. Spoon equal amounts of mixture into green peppers until gone. Place peppers in a small roasting pan and pour tomato sauce over tops. Bake in preheated oven for 45 minutes. Sprinkle cheese on top and bake an additional 15 minutes.

6 servings

Q: What did Violet do when George gave her money to help her out?

$45-a-Week Meat Loaf Surprise

2 pounds ground round
2 eggs
1 large potato, peeled and grated
½ cup dried bread crumbs
1 medium onion, chopped fine
Salt and pepper to taste
1 garlic clove, minced
1 (8-ounce) can tomato sauce
⅓ cup dark brown sugar
¼ cup distilled white vinegar
1 tablespoon ketchup
1 teaspoon prepared mustard

Preheat oven to 400 degrees F. In a large mixing bowl, combine first 7 ingredients and mix well. In a separate mixing bowl, combine remaining ingredients. Add half the sauce to meat mixture. Shape meat mixture into a loaf and place in a shallow baking pan. Pour half the remaining sauce over loaf. Bake in preheated oven for 45 minutes. Pour remainder of sauce over meat and serve.

8 to 10 servings

Mrs. Welch's Quick Beef and Noodles

1 medium onion, chopped fine
2 tablespoons butter or margarine
1 pound ground sirloin
1 (10¾ ounce) can condensed cream of mushroom soup
Salt and pepper to taste
Pinch of garlic powder
1 cup water
Cooked noodles, to suit

In a large skillet, over medium heat, sauté onions in butter. Add meat and cook until well browned. Stir in soup, seasonings, and water. Bring to a boil. Reduce heat and simmer, covered, for 15 minutes, or until thicker. Serve over cooked noodles.

4 to 6 servings

***A:** She kissed him, which left a big lipstick mark on his face.*

Secondhand Suitcase Sloppy Joes

1 pound ground round
1 small onion, chopped fine
2 tablespoons butter or margarine
1 garlic clove, minced
3 tablespoons ketchup
1 tablespoon prepared mustard
1 (10¾ ounce) can chicken gumbo soup
1 cup water
1 (3-ounce) can mushrooms
Salt and pepper to taste
Hamburger buns

In a large skillet, over medium heat, brown meat and onion in butter. Add all other ingredients except buns and stir. Bring to a boil. Reduce heat and simmer, covered, for about 30 minutes. Serve on hamburger buns.

8 servings

Mrs. Martini's Creamy Linguine

2 tablespoons butter
2 tablespoons flour
1 cup milk
Pinch of salt
½ teaspoon garlic powder
½ teaspoon dried parsley
½ cup grated Parmesan cheese
¼ cup shredded Mozzarella cheese
Linguine or fettuccine noodles to suit
Parmesan cheese for topping

In a saucepan, over medium heat, melt butter and add flour, stirring constantly until thick. Add milk and heat through, stirring continuously. Stir in remaining ingredients except noodles. Cook over medium heat until cheeses are completely melted and mixture thickens. Pour over cooked noodles and toss until well coated. Top with sprinklings of Parmesan. *Great as a small main dish or as a side dish.*

4 to 6 servings

Q: What was the name of the dance hall Violet was hauled out of in Pottersville?

Martini's "O Sole Mio" Spaghetti

1 pound ground chuck
1 large onion, chopped fine
1 garlic clove, crushed
1½ cups water
Salt and pepper to taste
½ teaspoon sugar
1 tablespoon oregano
½ teaspoon basil
½ teaspoon marjoram
1 (8-ounce) can tomato sauce
1 (6-ounce) can tomato paste
Cooked spaghetti noodles, to suit
Grated Parmesan cheese, to suit

In a large skillet, over medium heat, brown meat; drain off excess fat. Add onion and garlic and cook until tender; about 5 minutes. In a large dutch oven, combine hamburger and all other ingredients except spaghetti and Parmesan. Bring to a boil, over medium heat, stirring occasionally. Reduce heat and simmer, covered, for 1½ hours, or until thick. (Stir occasionally to mix everything well.) Serve sauce over cooked spaghetti noodles. Top with Parmesan cheese. *Best if served with a hot loaf of Italian bread.*

4 to 6 servings

Bootlegger's Wife Ritzy Chicken

4 small boneless chicken breasts, halved (8 fillets)
Salt and pepper to taste
Plain yogurt
1 sleeve Ritz crackers, crushed (or more if needed)
8 tablespoons butter or margarine
1 tablespoon parsley

Preheat oven to 325 degrees F. Remove all skin and excess fat from chicken breast halves and sprinkle with seasonings. Pour

---

***A:** Dime a Dance.*

yogurt in a small bowl. Put crushed crackers on a plate. Dip each chicken piece in yogurt until well coated. Roll chicken in crackers and place in a greased 9×13-inch baking pan. Melt butter in a small saucepan; add parsley. Pour mixture over chicken pieces. Bake, uncovered, in preheated oven for about an hour.

8 servings

The Martinis' Housewarming Lasagne Feast

1 pound ground beef-sausage mixture
2 tablespoons butter or margarine
1 small onion, chopped fine
1 garlic clove, minced
Salt and pepper to taste
1 (16-ounce) can tomatoes
2 (6-ounce) cans tomato paste
2 eggs, beaten
3 cups fresh ricotta cheese
½ cup grated Parmesan cheese
2 tablespoons parsley flakes
1 pound mozzarella cheese, shredded
½ cup shredded Cheddar cheese
12 lasagne noodles, cooked

Preheat oven to 375 degrees F. In a large skillet, over medium heat, brown meat, drain off excess fat. Add onion and garlic and cook until tender. Add salt and pepper, tomatoes, and tomato paste. Bring to a boil. Reduce heat and simmer, uncovered, for 15 minutes, stirring often. In a mixing bowl, add beaten eggs, ricotta cheese, Parmesan cheese, parsley, and salt and pepper; mix well. In a separate bowl, mix mozzarella and Cheddar cheese. In a 13×9×2-inch baking dish, layer one-third of the noodles. Spread one-third of the ricotta filling mixture on top, followed by one-third of the cheese mixture and one-third of the meat sauce. Repeat this process until done. Bake in preheated oven for 30 minutes. *Serve with fresh bread and your favorite wine.*

12 servings

Q: What was Emil Gower's son's name, and how did Mr. Gower's son die?

Mr. Carter's Home in Elmira Chicken Breast Casserole

This meal is easy to make—and tasty too.

4 boneless chicken breast halves
Salt and pepper to taste
Garlic powder to taste
1 (10¾-ounce) can condensed cream of mushroom soup
¼ soup can water
2 stalks celery, sliced
2 medium carrots, sliced
2 medium potatoes, peeled and sliced
1 medium onion, sliced
Butter dollops

Preheat oven to 375 degrees F. Remove all skin and excess fat from chicken breast halves and sprinkle with seasonings. Pour soup and water into a large casserole dish and mix. Place chicken on top of soup. Add all vegetables and place small dollops of butter on top of chicken. Cover and bake in preheated oven for 1 hour, or until potatoes are tender.

4 servings

Friday Fish With the Baileys

1 pound cod or perch fillets, cut into portions
Salt and pepper to taste
3 tablespoons butter or margarine, melted
1½ tablespoons lemon juice
½ teaspoon onion powder
Pinch of garlic powder
½ teaspoon dried parsley

***A:** His son was named Robert; he died from influenza.*

Preheat oven to 350 degrees F. Season both sides of fish with salt and pepper. Mix butter, lemon juice, onion powder, garlic powder, and parsley. Dip fillets into butter mixture and place in an ungreased 9×9×2-inch baking pan. Pour remaining butter mixture over fillets. Bake, uncovered, in preheated oven about 25 minutes, or until fish flakes easily with a fork. *This is great served with hush puppies and a baked potato!*

4 servings

Henry Potter Pot Pie

1 small boneless chicken breast, skinned, (about ¾ pound)
Salt and pepper to taste
1 tablespoon butter or margarine
2 ready-made 9-inch piecrusts
1 large potato, peeled and diced
2 medium carrots, sliced
½ cup peas, well drained
½ stalk celery, chopped
1 (10¾-ounce) can condensed cream of chicken soup

Preheat oven to 350 degrees F. Cut chicken breast into bite-size pieces and sprinkle with seasonings. In a skillet, over medium heat, melt butter and cook chicken just until it turns color on all sides. Remove from pan. Take one of the ready-made piecrusts and gently press it into a 9-inch pie pan. In a mixing bowl, combine chicken, potato, carrots, peas, celery, and soup. Pour mixture into pie shell. Place second piecrust over top. Trim edges and crimp. Cut small slits in top of crust. Bake in preheated oven for 30 minutes, or until crust is golden brown and juice is bubbly.

4 servings

Q: What happened that made George go to his dad's office?

Bailey Boys Chicken and Dumplings

This meal is very hearty, and great with mashed potatoes and fresh vegetables. Have your butcher cut up the chickens into individual serving pieces.

1 tablespoons butter or margarine
1 large onion, chopped fine
1 teaspoon cayenne pepper
5 tablespoons paprika
2 broiler-fryer chickens, cut up (about 18 pieces)
Salt and pepper to taste
2 tablespoons cornstarch
⅓ cup water
16 ounces sour cream
4 large eggs, beaten
Approximately 4 heaping tablespoons all-purpose flour

In a soup pot, over medium heat, sauté onions in butter. Add cayenne and paprika, and stir until well mixed. Add chicken pieces and enough water to cover completely. Add salt and pepper to taste. Bring to a boil. Reduce heat and let simmer, covered, for 1¼ hours, stirring occasionally. In a tightly closed container, shake together cornstarch and the ⅓ cup water. Bring chicken mixture to a slow boil. Add sour cream, stir well. Add small amounts of cornstarch mixture until desired thickness is obtained (it shouldn't be too thick!). Remove from heat. In a large dutch oven, bring 4 quarts water to a slow boil. In a small mixing bowl, combine eggs and flour to a creamy consistency. Drop teaspoonfuls of batter in the boiling water, cooking until they float to the top. Remove dumplings from water and add to chicken mixture. Heat mixture to desired temperature and serve.

8 to 10 servings

***A:** George discovered that Gower accidentally put poison in some capsules.*

South Pacific Honeymoon Chicken

Although this recipe calls for an electric wok, you can cook the chicken in a large skillet.

1-pound boneless chicken breast, skinned
2 tablespoons butter or margarine
½ medium green bell pepper, cut into pieces
½ medium sweet red bell pepper, cut into pieces
Salt and pepper to taste
2 (8-ounce) cans pineapple, undrained
½ cup water
1 tablespoons dark brown sugar
1 tablespoon honey
2 tablespoons soy sauce
1 teaspoon ground ginger
2 tablespoons cornstarch
Cooked rice

Cut chicken into strips. Set electric wok to stir-fry setting. Melt butter and sauté chicken and peppers only until chicken turns color. Add salt and pepper, pineapple with liquid, water, brown sugar, honey, soy sauce, and ginger. Stirfry until chicken is thoroughly cooked. Shake cornstarch and ¼ cup water in a tightly closed container. Gradually stir into chicken mixture until desired thickness is reached. Serve over cooked rice.

4 servings

Q: What gift did Gower buy George for his trip to Paris?

Up the River Without a Paddle Salmon Patties

1 (16-ounce) can salmon, well drained and flaked
1 egg, beaten
½ cup finely chopped onion
⅓ cup finely chopped green bell pepper
1 large carrot, chopped fine
½ cup saltine cracker crumbs
1 tablespoon flour
1 tablespoon lemon juice
Salt and pepper to taste
Vegetable oil

In a large mixing bowl, combine all ingredients except oil and mix well. Form into six patties. Heat a small amount of oil in a large skillet, over medium heat. Fry patties until golden brown on both sides, about 5 minutes per side, turning once. *Great with tartar sauce, ketchup, or cocktail sauce.*

6 servings

Nick the Bartender's Beer Batter Fish

1 pound perch fillets, halved
¾ cup stale beer
3 heaping tablespoons flour
3 tablespoons cornmeal
3 tablespoons lemon juice
1 egg
Salt and pepper to taste
Vegetable oil
1 lemon, cut into wedges
Potato chips or french fries
Vinegar or tartar sauce (optional)

About 3 hours before preparing fish, pour beer in a large mixing bowl to let it become stale. Dry fish fillets; set aside. In the

---

***A:** He bought George a large monogrammed suitcase.*

mixing bowl that contains the beer, mix in flour, cornmeal, lemon juice, egg, and salt and pepper to taste. Beat until very smooth. Put all fish fillets in batter and marinate for 20 minutes. Put 1-inch of oil in a dutch oven or large skillet; heat over medium heat. Using tongs, slowly dip the fillets into the hot oil. Fry a few at a time without crowding, until both sides are brown, turning once, about 5 minutes. (Be careful! Batter may spatter.) Drain on paper towels. Squeeze lemon juice on top. Serve with potato chips or french fries. *Hint: If you prefer french fries, it's easier to make them first and keep them warm while preparing the fish. Also, you can substitute malt vinegar for lemon juice for an authentic English taste.*

4 servings

George Bailey's "The One That Got Away" Tahitian Swordfish Steaks

2½–3 pounds swordfish steaks
¼ cup lemon juice
Salt and pepper to taste
1 teaspoon garlic powder
¼ cup water
¼ cup olive oil
3 tablespoons butter
1 teaspoon garlic powder

Preheat oven to 450 degrees F. Place swordfish steaks in a shallow baking dish and brush all the lemon juice on them. Sprinkle steaks with salt, pepper, and garlic powder; let stand for 15 minutes. In a small mixing bowl, blend water and oil. Brush the mixture over steaks. Bake in preheated oven, uncovered, for about 30 minutes, or until meat flakes easily with a fork. Brush with pan drippings 2 or 3 times during baking time. In a small saucepan, melt butter and mix in garlic powder. Stir well and serve in individual containers to each person, for dipping.

6 servings

Q: What was Clarence Oddbody's profession on Earth?

Little Zuzu's Cheesy Shrimp Pie

1 (8-ounce) container refrigerator crescent roll dough
1 cup shredded Monterey Jack cheese
½ cup shredded Cheddar cheese
2 eggs, beaten
1 (16-ounce) package frozen cocktail shrimp, thawed
¼ cup finely chopped onion
Salt and pepper to taste
Cocktail sauce

Preheat oven to 350 degrees F. Spread crescent roll dough in an 8-inch pie pan to form crust, trimming away edges. In a large mixing bowl, combine all ingredients except cocktail sauce and mix well. Pour filling into piecrust. Bake in preheated oven for about 50 to 60 minutes, or until firm throughout. Serve with coctail sauce.

6 servings

George Bailey Lassos Pork?

4-pound boneless pork top loin roast
Salt and pepper to taste
2½ cups water
½ teaspoon ground sage
2 garlic cloves, minced
2 large onions, quartered
4–5 medium potatoes, peeled and halved
8–10 medium carrots, peeled
2 tablespoons flour
¼ cup water

Preheat oven to 350 degrees F. Season pork with salt and pepper. Place pork in a roasting pan. In a mixing bowl, mix water, sage, and garlic. Pour mixture in bottom of roasting pan. Roast, uncovered, in preheated oven for 30 minutes. Remove pan from

---

***A:** He was a clockmaker.*

oven and baste roast with liquid. Add onions, cover, and return to oven for 1 hour at same temperature. Remove from oven and add potatoes and carrots. (Add more water if necessary.) Cook, covered, for 1 hour, or until done throughout. Remove meat from pan and place on serving platter, arranging vegetables around it. Skim off excess fat in pan. Shake flour and water in a tightly closed container and gradually stir into pan liquid. Heat to desired thickness and serve over meal.

8 to 10 servings

Exotic Wedding Night Luau Roast

Salt and pepper to taste
2½–3 pound pork shoulder
1 5½-ounce can crushed pineapple, with juice
¼ cup olive oil
¼ cup dark corn syrup
2 tablespoons lemon juice
1 garlic clove, minced
2 tablespoons brown sugar
2 teaspoons prepared mustard
2 teaspoons soy sauce
½ teaspoon ground ginger

Season pork and place in a large casserole dish. In a medium mixing bowl, combine remaining ingredients and pour over meat. Cover dish and let stand in refrigerator 6 to 8 hours, turning occasionally.

Preheat oven to 325 degrees F. Remove pork from casserole dish and place on a baking rack in a roasting pan. Strain pineapple chunks from marinade and spread on top of meat. Sprinkle ¼ cup of remaining marinade on meat. Roast, uncovered, in preheated oven for about 2½ hours, or until roast reaches an internal temperature of 170 degrees F. on a meat thermometer, basting occasionally with marinade.

8 to 10 servings

Q: What was Clarence's angel rank?

Bedford Falls Famous Barbecued Country Ribs

Boneless pork country ribs, 2 per person
Olive oil
1–2 cups barbecue sauce
1 small onion, chopped fine
Salt and pepper to taste
Mrs. Dash to taste
Garlic powder to taste

INDOORS: Preheat oven to 350 degrees F. Parboil ribs until tender, about 20 to 25 minutes. Place in a baking dish large enough to accomodate the ribs without crowing. In a small mixing bowl, mix barbecue sauce, onion, and all seasonings, and pour over pork. Bake, uncovered, in preheated oven for 30 minutes.

OUTDOORS: This is the best method! In a small mixing bowl, mix olive oil and seasonings. Brush generously on meat and let stand for 20 minutes. Get your barbecue fired up and place ribs on rack. Turn ribs as they become done on each side, about 20 to 25 minutes. In a small bowl, mix barbecue sauce and onion. Brush sauce generously on each side and cook an additional 5 minutes, turning once. Since this is pork, make sure the ribs are cooked through. *The smell of this meal will drive your neighbors wild! Great with baked potato and green beans.*

Serves any number, depending on number of ribs

Potter's Pork-Barrel Pork Chops

4 boneless pork chops, halved
Salt and pepper to taste
Mrs. Dash to taste
Garlic powder to taste
2 eggs
1 cup Italian-style bread crumbs
1 small onion, sliced
Vegetable oil

***A:** He was Angel Second Class.*

Preheat oven to 350 degrees F. Season meat with all seasonings; let stand. In a small bowl, beat eggs well. Place bread crumbs on a large plate. Place ½ inch vegetable oil in a large skillet; heat over medium heat. Dip each piece of meat into egg, then into bread crumbs, until well coated. Brown each piece in vegetable oil, turning once. Place 2 halves side by side on a large piece of aluminum foil, and place a quarter of the onion on top. Seal into pouchlike shape. Place pouches on a baking sheet and place in preheated oven. Bake for 1 hour. Remove meat from foil pouches and serve.

4 servings

Mary's "I'll Love You Till the Day I Die" Veal Steak

1½ pounds fresh veal round steak, quartered
Salt and pepper to taste
Mrs. Dash to taste
Garlic powder to taste
2 eggs
1 cup Italian-style bread crumbs
1 small onion, sliced
Vegetable oil
1 (10¾-ounce) can tomato soup
1 tablespoon flour (or more)

Preheat oven to 350 degrees F. Season meat with all seasonings; let stand. In a small bowl, beat eggs well. Place bread crumbs on a large plate. Place ½ inch of vegetable oil in a large skillet; heat over medium heat. Dip each piece of meat into egg, then into bread crumbs, until well coated. Brown each piece in vegetable oil, turning once. Place each piece of meat on a large piece of aluminum foil, and place quarter of the onion on top. Seal into pouchlike shape. Place pouches on a baking sheet and place in preheated oven. Bake for 1 hour. Remove from foil pouches. In a small saucepan, over medium heat, heat tomato soup. Gradually stir in 1 tablespoon flour until thick. (Use more if necessary.) *Spoon soup mixture over meat and mashed potatoes.*

4 servings

Q: What book was Clarence reading in heaven?

Ernie Bishop's Wartime Cordon Bleu

1 pound veal round steak, quartered
Salt and pepper to taste
4 thin slices honey-smoked ham
4 thin slices Swiss cheese
2 eggs
1 cup dried bread crumbs
3 tablespoons vegetable oil
3 tablespoons water
Cooked noodles

Lay each slice of veal on a cutting board. Season as desired and place one slice of ham and 1 slice of cheese on each. Roll up meat and secure with toothpicks. Beat eggs in a small bowl. Pour bread crumbs on large plate. Heat oil in a 10-inch skillet over medium heat. Dip rolled meat in egg and then in bread crumbs, until well coated. Cook rolls until golden brown on all sides, turning as needed. Add water to skillet. Bring to a boil. Reduce heat and simmer, covered, for 45 minutes. For crisper veal, remove cover for last 5 minutes. *Serve with buttered noodles and favorite vegetable.*

4 servings

Mary Had a Little Lamb Chops

3 tablespoons olive oil
Salt and pepper to taste
Garlic powder to taste
4 to 6 lamb chops, 1 inch thick (loin or sirloin)
¼ cup honey
¼ cup prepared mustard

Preheat broiler. In a small bowl, combine olive oil and seasonings. Brush each lamb chop with oil mixture and make slits in fat to help prevent curling. In a small saucepan, over medium heat,

---

***A:** He was reading* The Adventures of Tom Sawyer.

combine honey and mustard; heat until warm. Place chops on rack in broiler pan. Place pan under broiler, so that chops are 3 inches from heat. Broil until slightly brown; brush with sauce. Finish browning first side; turn. Repeat for second side. (Cook about 7 minutes per side.) Pour leftover sauce over chops.

4 to 6 servings

Poor in Pottersville Vegetable Lasagne

3 tablespoons olive oil
½ cup finely chopped onion
3 garlic cloves, chopped fine
1½ cups carrot, finely chopped
1½ cups cream
Salt and pepper to taste
3 tablespoons flour
1 (16-ounce) package frozen broccoli pieces, thawed
2 cups Ricotta cheese
½ cup grated Parmesan cheese
2 eggs, beaten
⅓ cup chopped fresh parsley
2 cups shredded Mozzarella cheese
12 lasagne noodles, cooked

Preheat oven to 350 degrees F. In a medium saucepan, over medium heat, sauté onions, garlic, and carrot until tender. Add cream, seasonings, and flour. Cook over low heat until thickened. Stir in broccoli. In a separate bowl, combine Ricotta, Parmesan, eggs, and parsley; mix well. Place 4 noodles in a casserole dish. Spread one-third of the broccoli mixture on top, followed by one-third of the cheese-egg mixture, and one-third of the Mozzarella. Repeat twice more. Bake, uncovered, in preheated oven for about 1¼ to 1½ hours, until bubbly. Let cool awhile before serving.

10 to 12 servings

Q: How old was Clarence when he met George Bailey?

Ruth Dakin-Bailey's Nickel-and-Dime Cube Steak

4 cube steaks
Salt and pepper to taste
Garlic powder to taste
Flour
2 tablespoons butter or margarine
1 (10¾-ounce) can condensed cream of mushroom soup
½ soup can water
1 medium onion, sliced
2 medium potatoes, peeled and sliced
3 medium carrots, sliced
2 stalks celery, sliced

Preheat oven to 350 degrees F. Season cube steaks to your liking. Sprinkle each piece with flour on both sides. In a large skillet, over medium heat, melt butter and brown meat, turning once. Pour soup and water in a large casserole dish and mix well. Add in all vegetables, then place meat on top. Spoon some of the mixture on top of meat. Cook, covered, in preheated oven for 1 hour.

4 servings

Atsa Some Pizza Pie!

Cornmeal
1 recipe pizza dough (recipe in Bread section; see index)
1 (15-ounce) can tomato sauce
1 teaspoon oregano
½ teaspoon dried parsley
½ teaspoon basil
Pinch of pepper
2 cups shredded Mozzarella cheese
1 cup sliced pepperoni
Mushroom slices, as you like
Green bell pepper slices, as you like
Onion slices, as you like
Chopped ham, as you like

***A:** He was 292 years old.*

Preheat oven to 375 degrees F. Before placing dough on pizza pan, sprinkle pan with cornmeal. Stretch dough and place on pan. In a bowl, combine tomato sauce, herbs, and peppers; spread evenly over dough. Spread cheese evenly over sauce, followed by pepperoni. The beauty of this meal is that you can create your own toppings! Add whatever you like on top. Once prepared, bake pizza in preheated oven until crust turns golden brown and cheese is fully melted, about 15 to 20 minutes.

6 servings

Brunch at the Baileys' Potato-Noodle Hash

6 small potatoes, washed, peeled, and sliced (okay to leave unpeeled if you prefer)
1½ cups coarsely crushed noodles (use your hand)
3 tablespoons butter or margarine (or more)
1 small onion, chopped fine
6 bacon slices, cooked and crumbled
4 eggs
Salt and pepper to taste

Place potatoes in a medium saucepan, cover with water, and boil until tender; drain well. While potatoes are cooking, cook noodles in a separate pan, according to package directions; drain well. Cut potatoes into bite-sized pieces. Heat 3 tablespoons butter in a large skillet over medium heat and sauté onion until tender. Add potatoes and noodles and cook until some begin to crisp, stirring so no burning occurs. (Add more butter if necessary.) Add bacon. In a medium bowl, beat eggs and pour over potato mixture, stirring constantly until egg is completely cooked. Salt and pepper to taste.

6 servings

Q: What did Clarence order in the bar?

Saturday Barbecue With the Baileys

Ground round for hamburgers (figure 3 or 4 per pound)
Hot dogs
Hamburger and hot dog buns
1 medium onion, sliced
1 small onion, chopped fine
1 tomato, sliced
¼ head iceberg lettuce, separated into leaves
1 (16-ounce) jar dill pickles
Condiments, as desired
1 or 2 large bag chips
Sodas for everyone

Divide hamburger into patties and place on large plate, putting wax paper in between. Put hot dogs on separate plate. Fire up the barbecue!

Arrange sliced onion, chopped onion, tomato, lettuce leaves, and pickles on a serving tray. Gather condiments as desired. Grab the chips and sodas, and head for the back yard! Cook meat until desired state of crispness is achieved and enjoy family games.

Serves as many as desired.

U.S.O. Club Sandwich

12 slices white or whole-wheat bread
Mayonnaise or salad dressing to suit
8 lettuce leaves
4 slices cooked chicken or turkey
8 slices tomato
12 slices crisp bacon

Toast bread slices. Spread mayonnaise on 4 slices. In layers, add half the lettuce, the chicken, and another slice of toast each. In more layers, add remaining lettuce, tomato, and bacon slices. Spread remaining slices of toast with mayonnaise and top off the sandwiches. Secure with toothpicks and cut diagonally. *Serve with pickles and potato chips.*

4 servings

***A:** He ordered mulled wine, heavy on the cinnamon, light on the cloves.*

The World's Best P-B-J Sandwich!

This recipe was given by Jimmy Hawkins, who played Tommy Bailey in It's a Wonderful Life. *As it happens, little Jimmy didn't like eating the food at studio commissaries, so his mother would pack him his favorite lunch, a peanut butter and jelly sandwich! For those on a diet, substitute with sourdough bread, low-fat apricot jelly, and skim milk.*

Skippy peanut butter
2 slices Wonder bread
Boisenberry jelly
Milk
Fritos

Put a good amount of Skippy on 1 slice Wonder Bread. Put an equal amount of boisenberry jelly on the other. Add a glass of whole milk and a generous helping of Fritos, and there you have the world's greatest lunch!

1 serving

Bailey Family Off-to-School Early-Riser Egg Sandwich

1 tablespoon butter or margarine
1 egg
Mayonnaise or salad dressing
2 slices favorite bread (toasted, if desired)
1 slice cheese
1 slice tomato (optional)
Lettuce leaf (optional)

In a small skillet, over medium heat, melt butter and add egg. Burst yolk so it spills over. Cook until done, flipping once. Spread mayonnaise on 1 slice of bread and top with cheese. Add egg and top with tomato, lettuce, and bread. *Great for people on the go!*

1 serving

Q: How was Henry Potter referred to by George Bailey?

Harry Bailey Hero Sandwich

1 onion roll or submarine roll
Mayonnaise or salad dressing
1 slice Swiss cheese
2 slices ham
2 slices turkey
2 slices bologna
2 slices salami
1 slice Muenster cheese
1 slice American cheese
3 lettuce leaves
1 tablespoon very finely chopped onion
Mustard

Slice roll in half. On the bottom half, spread a generous amount of mayonnaise. In layers, add Swiss cheese, one slice each of ham, turkey, bologna, and salami, and Muenster cheese. Add lettuce and onion. In more layers, add remaining meat and American cheese. Spread mustard on top half of bun and secure sandwich with toothpicks. Cut in half. *Serve with pickles and chips and you have the perfect sandwich for any hero!*

1 serving

Spaghetti alla Carbonara

Here's another great recipe from Argentina Brunetti, but certainly not as hot as the first one. Argentina says, "Buon Appetito!"

4 eggs, lightly beaten
½ cup grated Parmesan cheese
3 tablespoons olive oil
1 (6-ounce) package smoked Canadian bacon
Hot peppers, as you like, chopped
2 pounds cooked spaghetti (al dente please)

***A:** George called him a warped, frustrated old man.*

In a mixing bowl, whip eggs and add Parmesan cheese; mix well. Set aside. In a large skillet, over medium heat, heat olive oil and cook Canadian bacon. Add hot peppers as you like. While this is cooking, cook spaghetti according to package directions; drain well. As soon as spaghetti is drained, add to skillet with bacon and add egg mixture. Stir over medium heat for about 1 minute, or until eggs are cooked through and cheese is melted.

4 to 6 servings

Mother Minnie Mueller's Macaroni and Hamburger

This recipe was given by Carol Coombs Mueller, who played Janie Bailey in the movie. This recipe is from her mother-in-law, Minnie Mueller. Carol is a retired schoolteacher, and, yes, she really did play "Hark, The Herald Angels Sing" in the movie!

2 tablespoons butter or margarine
1½ pounds lean ground beef
1 large onion, chopped fine
2 garlic cloves, minced
1½ cups elbow macaroni
Salt and pepper to taste

In a large skillet, over medium heat, heat butter and brown meat, breaking it up until it crumbles. Add onion and garlic and cook until tender. In a saucepan, cook macaroni according to package directions; drain. Combine meat and macaroni in a large mixing bowl and season to taste.

OPTIONAL: *Add ¾ cup ketchup or 1 (6-ounce) can of tomato sauce.*

4 to 6 servings

Q: What did Potter want to do with the Bailey Building & Loan after Peter Bailey died?

Brunetti's Penne all'Arrabiatta (Hot Pasta!)

This spicy recipe was given by Argentina Brunetti, who played Mrs. Martini in the film. Argentina lives in California and is very active writing for several Italian newspapers. Buon appetito!

8 tablespoons extra virgin olive oil
2 jalapeño peppers, chopped fine
4 garlic cloves, minced
2 (15-ounce) cans tomato sauce
2 tablespoons chopped fresh parsley
Cooked spaghetti, to suit

In a dutch oven, over medium heat, heat olive oil and sauté peppers and garlic until golden. Add tomato sauce and cook for 25 minutes, stirring often. Add parsley before serving. Pour over cooked spaghetti.

4 to 6 servings

***A:** He wanted to dissolve it.*

Side Dishes

"Donna had a chance to speak to Frank Capra in early 1982 at a salute held in his honor by the American Film Institute. Capra said that if he could change one thing about the film, he would have portrayed Mary as stronger and more attractive, instead of drab and weak, in the nonexistent-George section of the film. Donna always had a great deal of respect for Capra, and this touched her very deeply."

—*Grover Asmus* (Donna Reed's widower)

Zuzu's All-Time-Favorite Cheesy Grits

This is one of my very favorite side dishes!

1½ cups fast-cooking grits
5 cups water
Salt and pepper to taste
1 pound Cheddar cheese, shredded
¾ cup (1½ sticks) butter or margarine
3 eggs, lightly beaten

Preheat oven to 350 degrees F. In a saucepan, cook grits, with water, and salt and pepper, according to package directions. When grits are cooked and still hot, add all the other ingredients. Stir well and pour into greased 2 quart casserole dish. Bake uncovered in preheated oven for 1 hour.

6 to 8 servings

Hotter Than the Boardroom Baked Potatoes

As many potatoes as needed
8 tablespoons (1 stick) butter or margarine, melted
Salt and pepper to taste
Garlic powder to taste
Butter or margarine for topping
Finely chopped chives
Sour cream, as needed

Preheat oven to 375 degrees F. Wash potatoes well. Cut 2 small slits in each potato, then cook all at once in microwave on HIGH for 7 minutes. Add seasonings to melted butter. Cut aluminum foil wrapping for each potato. As you take potatoes from the microwave, brush each with good amount of butter and spices and wrap in aluminum foil. Cook in preheated oven for 50 minutes, or until skins are slightly crisp. Top with butter, chives, and sour cream.

Serves as many as desired

Q: What kind of employment contract did Potter offer George?

Capra-Style Gnocchi alla Cheddar

3 cups milk
8 tablespoons (1 stick) butter or margarine
1 teaspoon salt
¾ cup fast-cooking Cream of Wheat
2 cups shredded Cheddar cheese
1 egg, lightly beaten

In a saucepan, combine 2 cups milk, half of the butter, and salt and bring to a boil over medium heat. Add Cream of Wheat to remaining milk, stir, and add to heated mixture. Cook until thickened, stirring constantly. Remove from heat and add 1 cup cheese and the egg, and blend well. Pour into a greased 8×10-inch baking pan and chill for 1 hour.

Preheat oven to 425 degrees F. Cut into small squares and arrange in a shallow baking dish. Melt remaining butter and pour over top. Sprinkle buttered squares with remaining cheese. Bake in preheated oven for 25 to 35 minutes, or until cheese is melted and lightly browned.

8 servings

Mrs. Welch's Mind Your Peas and Carrots Rice

Cooked instant rice (as much as needed)
1 cup frozen peas and carrots
Salt and pepper to taste
1 tablespoon butter or margarine

Prepare as much instant rice as needed, according to package instructions. Fork all rice into a serving bowl. Meantime, cook frozen peas and carrots per package instruction and gently mix with rice. Salt and pepper to taste. Put butter on top just before serving.

2 cups of cooked rice = 6 servings

***A:** A three-year contract at $20,000 per year to manage his properties.*

Violet Bick's Always Creamy Rice

1 (10¾-ounce) can condensed cream of chicken soup (any "cream of" soup will work—your choice!)
1 soup can instant rice, uncooked
Salt and pepper to taste

In a small saucepan, over low to medium heat, heat creamy soup without adding water. While soup is heating, clean and dry inside of can. Pour in enough rice to fill can. When soup is really hot, stir in rice. Remove from heat, cover, and let stand for 5 to 7 minutes. Salt and pepper to taste.

4 servings

J. W. Hatch's Mealtime Rice

8-ounces very fine egg noodles (uncooked)
1 cup (2 sticks) butter or margarine, melted
2 (10¾-ounce) cans chicken broth
2 (10¾-ounce) cans onion soup
2 cups uncooked instant rice
1 cup warm water
1 (6-ounce) can sliced water chestnuts, drained
1 (4-ounce) can sliced mushrooms, drained

Preheat oven to 350 degrees F. In a skillet, over medium heat, brown noodles in melted butter. In a large mixing bowl, combine noodles with all other ingredients and blend. Pour into 3-quart casserole dish. Bake uncovered in preheated oven for about 45 minutes, or until bubbly.

6 to 8 servings

Q: What was Potter's job during World War II?

Harry Bailey's Spicy Dicey Ricey

This is another great recipe given by Todd Karns, who played Harry Bailey in the film.

1 medium onion, chopped fine
3 tablespoons butter or margarine
½ cup frozen peas, thawed
½ cup diced carrots
1 (8-ounce) can stewed tomatoes
1 (8-ounce) can tomato sauce
3 cups cooked instant rice
Salt and pepper to taste
Ground red pepper to taste

In a large skillet, over medium heat, sauté onion in butter until tender, about 5 minutes. Add all other ingredients. Simmer, uncovered, over low heat until hot, stirring occasionally. Add as much red pepper as your mouth can stand!

10 to 12 servings

Annie's Good-Anytime Fried Potatoes

6 medium potatoes
Vegetable oil
1 medium onion, sliced and separated into rings
Salt and pepper to taste
Mrs. Dash to taste (optional)

Wash potatoes before slicing. If you prefer them without skins, peel before rinsing. Slice potatoes ¼ inch thick. Dry thoroughly on paper towels. Cover the bottom of a large skillet with vegetable oil and heat, over medium heat. Arrange potatoes and onion in skillet and add seasonings. Lower heat and cook covered for 20 to 25 minutes, checking occasionally to see that potatoes are not burning. Flip as needed and cook until both sides are golden brown. (Add additional oil if needed.)

4 to 6 servings

***A:** Head of the draft board.*

I Want to Live Again Twice Baked Potatoes

Potatoes as needed
Cream cheese (1 tablespoon per potato)
Butter or margarine (1 teaspoon per potato)
Salt and pepper to taste
Milk as needed
Finely chopped chives, as desired
Cheddar cheese

Preheat oven to 375 degrees F. Wash potatoes well. Cut 2 small slits in each potato, then cook all at once in microwave on HIGH for 7 minutes. Bake potatoes in preheated oven for 30 minutes. Remove from oven and let stand for 15 minutes. Cut potatoes in half and scoop out insides, leaving a thin shell. In a mixing bowl, combine potato insides, cream cheese, butter, salt and pepper, milk, and chives, and mash until smooth. Spoon mixture into potato shells. Return potatoes to oven and bake, uncovered, until golden brown, about 15 to 20 minutes. Top with Cheddar cheese.

Serves as many as desired

Angel Fluff Mashed Potatoes

8 medium potatoes
½ cup milk (or more)
⅓ cup butter or margarine, plus more for garnish
2 tablespoons cream cheese
½ teaspoon salt
Pepper to taste

Peel potatoes and cut into small cubes. In a medium saucepan, place potatoes and enough water to cover. Boil for 15 minutes, or until tender; drain. Return potatoes to pan and mash with beater until few or no lumps are left. Add all other ingredients; beat with electric mixer at low speed until light and fluffy. Add more milk if needed to get desired consistency. Scoop into serving bowl and garnish with a dollop of butter.

6 to 8 servings

Q: What words did Potter say that made George want to commit suicide?

Mr. Martini's Italian Parmesan Potatoes

1/3 cup flour
1/3 cup grated Parmesan cheese
Salt and pepper to taste
Mrs. Dash to taste
6 medium potatoes, peeled and quartered
1/3 cup butter or margarine, melted

Preheat oven to 375 degrees F. In a large plastic zipper bag, combine flour, cheese, and seasonings. Dip potatoes in water and shake in bag until completely covered. (You might want to shake in 2 separate batches.) Put melted butter in a 9×13-inch baking pan and add potatoes. Bake, uncovered, in preheated oven for 20 minutes. Turn potatoes over and bake another 15 to 20 minutes, or until golden brown and slightly crisp.

5 to 6 servings

Violet's "Hot Patootie" Potato Pancakes

6 medium potatoes, peeled and grated
1 medium onion, grated
2 eggs
3 heaping tablespoons flour
Salt and pepper to taste
Vegetable oil
Sour cream
Applesauce

In a large mixing bowl, combine potatoes, onion, eggs, flour, and salt and pepper; mix well. Put enough vegetable oil in a large skillet to completely cover bottom; heat over medium to high heat. Drop potato mixture into hot oil by the small ladle. Fry until golden brown on bottom, about a minute. Flip and brown the other side, about another minute. Drain on paper towels. Serve with sour cream and applesauce.

14 to 16 servings

***A:** "You're worth more dead than alive."*

Karolyn's Cheese Potatoes

This is my version of a recipe given to me by Carol Coombs Mueller, who played Janie Bailey in the film. Carol is now a retirued schoolteacher. Enjoy!

2 (2-pound) bags frozen hash browns, thawed
1 (10¾-ounce) can condensed cream of chicken soup
¾ cup sour cream
2 cups grated Cheddar cheese
2 tablespoons finely chopped onion
Salt and pepper to taste
4 tablespoons butter or margarine, melted
1 cup corn flakes, crushed

Preheat oven to 350 degrees F. In a large mixing bowl, mix all ingredients except half the butter and corn flakes. Place into a 9×13-inch baking dish. Pour the remaining butter over the corn flakes and mix. Sprinkle corn flakes on top of potato mixture. Bake, uncovered, in preheated oven for 1 hour.

8 to 10 servings

Bailey Baked Beans and Bacon

1 pound bacon slices
1 large onion, chopped fine
3 (16-ounce) cans baked beans (your favorite choice)
3 tablespoons dark brown sugar
½ cup ketchup
1 tablespoon Worcestershire sauce
1 tablespoon prepared mustard

Preheat oven to 350 degrees F. In a large skillet, cook bacon until crisp; drain on paper towels and crumble. Reserve 4 tablespoons of bacon drippings. Heat these bacon drippings in a large pot, over medium heat, and sauté onions until tender. Add baked beans, brown sugar, ketchup, Worcestershire, mustard, and bacon; mix well. Pour into casserole dish and bake in preheated oven for 1½ hours.

12 to 14 servings

The town comes out to help George Bailey.

Vegetables

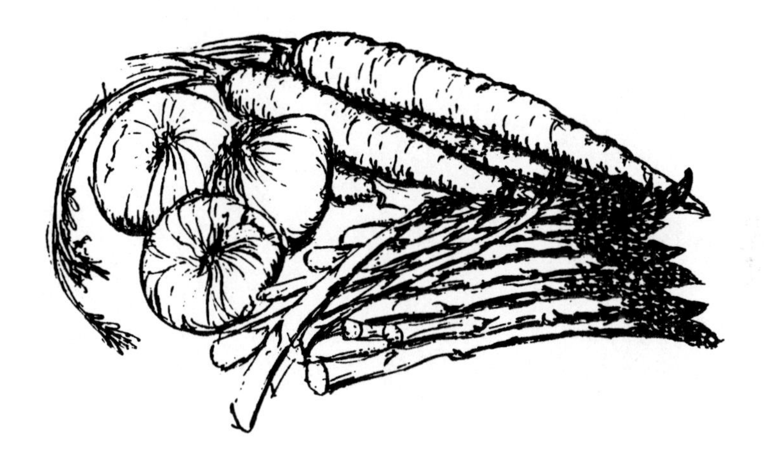

"I think this is one of the most watched films ever. People can't seem to help themselves once they know it's on! Maybe they're hoping that something nice might happen to them like it did for George Bailey. It's not just the happy ending either, it's the message of the whole film."

—*Argentina Brunetti* (Mrs. Martini)

Happy to be home again, George Bailey races down the stairs with family in tow.

Cooking Vegetables

Most vegetables are easy to cook—you just open the package from the freezer, stick them in water in a pot, and boil them. Many people top them with butter or margarine and serve. Try these variations to put a zip in your everyday vegetable dish.

- Try substituting Mrs. Dash for salt. A few sprinkles on corn, carrots, peas, or beans, and you won't even need butter! It's good on anything.
- Instead of boiling the vegetables, try steaming them. They'll stay crunchier, taste better, and retain many of the nutrients that are lost during boiling.
- Tired of just one kind of vegetable with your meal? Buy bags of several different kinds and create your own blends!
- Prepared vegetables store for a long time in freezer bags. Try diced carrots, peas, and chopped onion . . . cut-up broccoli, green beans, and onion . . . or a feisty blend of green, red, and yellow peppers with a dash of garlic.

Mr. Martini's "How 'bout Some Wine" Sauce Asparagus

2 (10-ounce) packages frozen asparagus tips
1/3 cup dry white wine
1 tablespoon finely chopped green onion, with tops
Pinch of thyme
3/4 cup mayonnaise
1/2 tablespoon lemon juice
1 garlic clove, finely chopped
2 eggs, hard boiled and chopped

Cook asparagus according to instructions on package; drain. Meantime, in a medium saucepan, combine wine, green onion, thyme, mayonnaise, lemon juice, and garlic. Bring to a slow boil over low heat and add eggs; stir gently. Pour hot over asparagus tips.

4 to 6 servings

Q: Who were the other employees at the Building & Loan?

Sweet as a Rose-Mary's Spinach

2 pounds spinach
¼ teaspoon fresh rosemary, minced
1 garlic clove, finely chopped
1 teaspoon dried parsley
¼ teaspoon dried basil
2 tablespoons butter
¼ cup water
Salt and pepper to taste

Wash spinach thoroughly and remove stems. Chop fine and place in large saucepan. Add rosemary, garlic, parsley, basil, butter, and water; cover. Cook over low to medium heat for about 15 minutes, or until tender, stirring occasionally. Add salt and pepper. Best if served hot!

4 to 6 servings

G.I. Wanna Come Home to Your Savory Spinach

1 (8-ounce) package frozen chopped spinach
1 (8-ounce) package cream cheese, softened
½ cup sour cream
2 small green onions, chopped fine
1 tablespoon horseradish
Salt and pepper to taste
⅓ cup dried bread crumbs
¼ cup melted butter or margarine

Preheat oven to 350 degrees F. Cook spinach according to package instructions; drain. Add softened cream cheese, sour cream, green onions, horseradish, salt, and pepper. Mix and pour into ungreased casserole dish. Sprinkle bread crumbs over top and pour butter over mixture. Bake in preheated oven for about 25 minutes, or until bubbly.

4 servings

***A:** Cousin Tillie and Cousin Eustace.*

Army Green Bean Casserole

2 (16-ounce) cans french-cut green beans, drained
1 (10¾-ounce) condensed cream of mushroom soup
½ cup milk
¼ cup shredded Cheddar cheese
Salt and pepper to taste
1 (16-ounce) can fried onions
1 tablespoon butter or margarine

Preheat oven to 350 degrees F. Place drained green beans in 2½ quart baking dish. In a medium bowl, mix soup and milk, and pour over green beans. Add Cheddar cheese. Salt and pepper to taste and sprinkle fried onions over top. Place butter in middle. Bake in preheated oven for 30 minutes, or until golden brown.

6 to 8 servings

Potter's Swiss Bank Account "Big Cheese" Green Beans

2 (16-ounce) cans green beans, drained
2 cups shredded Swiss cheese
2 tablespoons butter or margarine
2 tablespoons flour
1½ cups sour cream
1 small onion, chopped fine
Salt and pepper to taste
½ cup dried bread crumbs

Preheat oven to 375 degrees F. In a 2-quart casserole dish, place a layer of green beans, a layer of cheese, and repeat layers. Over low heat, melt butter in a medium saucepan. Add flour and blend. Add sour cream, onion, and salt and pepper. Cook until thick, stirring constantly. Pour sauce over green bean mixture. Sprinkle bread crumbs over top; bake in preheated oven for 20 minutes.

6 to 8 servings

Q: What phrase hung on the wall beneath Peter Bailey's picture at the office?

Our Boys in Brussels Sprouts

1 (16-ounce) package frozen Brussels sprouts
3/4 cup milk
2 cups shredded Cheddar cheese
3 slices American cheese, chopped
2 tablespoons butter or margarine
Salt and pepper to taste
1 tablespoon corn starch
1 tablespoon milk

In a medium saucepan, cook Brussels sprouts according to package directions until tender. Drain sprouts and return to pot. Add milk, cheeses, butter, and salt and pepper; cook over medium heat until cheeses are melted and well blended. Dissolve cornstarch in milk and slowly add to mixture. Reduce heat slightly and cook until cheese sauce is hot and thick.

4 servings

Copper Penny Carrots

14–16 carrots, peeled and sliced
2 medium onions, sliced and separated into rings
1 medium green bell pepper, sliced
1 (10 3/4-ounce) can condensed tomato soup
3/4 cup distilled white vinegar
2/3 cup sugar
1–2 tablespoons Worcestershire sauce
1 teaspoon prepared mustard
Salt and pepper to taste

In large saucepan, cook sliced carrots in boiling water until tender, about 20 minutes. Drain and combine with onions and green pepper in a serving bowl. Mix all other ingredients in a separate bowl, and pour over carrots. Cover and marinate in refrigerator overnight. Stir and serve. (Can be taken out 1/2 hour before serving to take chill off.)

7 to 8 servings

***A:** "All you can take with you is that which you've given away."*

"I'll Give You the Moon, Mary" Garden Delight Medley

For more flavor and crackle, steam these vegetables instead of boiling them.

1 head cauliflower
1 head broccoli
4 carrots, diced
½ small onion, chopped fine
½ medium sweet red bell pepper, chopped
2 tablespoons butter or margarine
Salt and pepper to taste

Break cauliflower head into small pieces, discarding stems; rinse thoroughly and drain. Do same to broccoli. In a large saucepan, cook cauliflower, broccoli, and carrots in water until tender. Drain; place in large serving bowl. In small skillet, sauté onions and red pepper in butter until tender, about 5 minutes. Pour mixture over vegetables. Salt and pepper to taste. *For extra zip, add 1 garlic clove, chopped fine, to sauté mixture, or sprinkle vegetables with Mrs. Dash.*

6 to 8 servings

Bedford Falls Corn Bake

Fresh corn on the cob, 2 ears per person
Butter or margarine, at room temperature
Salt and pepper

Preheat oven to 450 degrees F. Husk and wash each ear of corn. Spread with butter and season. Wrap each ear in aluminum foil and bake in preheated oven for 30 minutes. Turn 2 or 3 times during cooking.

Serves 2 ears per person
14 to 16 servings

Q: How much money did Tom want during the bank run?

Karolyn's Fourth of July Firecracker Summer Zucchini

After all, it is *my birthday!*

4 Italian plum tomatoes, blanched and peeled
2 tablespoons olive oil
1 medium garlic clove, chopped fine
1 small red onion, chopped fine
4 medium zucchini, sliced in half moons
2 dashes of Tabasco sauce

Blanch tomatoes by placing them in boiling water for 3 minutes; when just cool enough to handle, pop them out of their skins and set aside; discard the skins. In a large skillet, heat olive oil and sauté garlic and onion. Add zucchini, tomatoes, and Tabasco sauce. Simmer until zucchini is tender.

6 to 8 servings

Baked Zucchini alla Mr. Martini

4 eggs
3 medium zucchini, thinly sliced (about 3 cups)
1 cup baking/pancake mix
½ cup finely chopped onion
⅓ cup grated Parmesan cheese
1 tablespoon parsley
1 teaspoon Mrs. Dash or other seasoning mix
½ teaspoon garlic powder
½ cup vegetable oil

Preheat oven to 350 degrees F. Beat eggs in a large mixing bowl. Add all other ingredients and mix well. Pour into greased 2½-quart casserole dish. Bake in preheated oven for 30 minutes, or until golden brown. Cut into squares.

6 to 8 servings

***A:** Tom demanded $242.*

Ma Bailey's Summertime Vegetable Tray

1 head Iceberg lettuce
1 head celery
1 pound carrots
2 medium green bell peppers
1 large sweet red bell pepper
1 bunch radishes
2 bunches green onions
1 large cucumber
1 head broccoli
1 head cauliflower
1 (16-ounce) jar sweet pickles
1 (16-ounce) jar dill pickles

Layer a bed of lettuce on a very large serving platter, possibly two. Rinse and trim celery; cut stalks in half, then split 3 ways lengthwise; set aside. Peel carrots and slice into sticks; set aside. Rinse and core green and red peppers, slice into lengthwise strips; set aside. Wash and top radishes; set aside. Peel top layer off green onions, trim tops; set aside. Rinse cucumber, slice in half, cut lengthwise into strips; set aside. Break broccoli and cauliflower into small florets, discarding stems, rinse; set aside. Now that you have all these vegetables set aside, arrange them in a festive way on the platter(s), adding pickles. Chill, if desired. Serve with favorite dip, or by themselves. Serves a lot! Great for parties.

12 to 14 servings

Q: What took the place of the Building & Loan in Pottersville?

Seven Seas Glazed Carrots

12 large carrots
2 tablespoons butter or margarine
½ cup dark brown sugar, packed
Salt and pepper to taste
½ teaspoon grated orange or lemon peel
¼ cup walnuts, chopped
Celery leaves for garnish

Peel and top carrots; cut in half and split into quarters. Place carrots in a large saucepan with enough water to cover; bring to a boil. Reduce heat and simmer, covered, for 20 minutes. Drain carrots. In a large skillet, over medium heat, melt butter. Add brown sugar, salt and pepper, and peel; cook until bubbly. Add carrots and walnuts. Cook over low heat until carrots are heated and glazed. Garnish with celery leaves.

6 to 8 servings

Annie's Yummy for the Tummy Cheese-n-Broccoli Grits

1½ cups instant cheese grits
6 cups water
12 tablespoons (1½ sticks) butter
1 pound Cheddar cheese, grated
½ cup chopped broccoli florets
3 teaspoons Mrs. Dash or other seasoning mix
3 eggs

Preheat oven to 325 degrees F. In a medium saucepan, cook grits in water until mushy. Add butter, cheese, broccoli, and Mrs. Dash; mix well. Beat eggs and add to grits. Pour mixture into 9×13-inch casserole dish and bake in preheated oven for 1 hour.

6 to 8 servings

***A:** A nightclub called Dime a Dance.*

Ernie Bishop's More Than Fare Peas and Carrots Medley

1 (10-ounce) package frozen peas
4 carrots, peeled and diced
½ (6-ounce) jar baby onions or shallots
2 tablespoons butter or margarine
¼ teaspoon garlic powder
Salt and pepper to taste

Cook frozen peas according to package directions, with carrots. (Let cook an extra 5 minutes if softer carrots are desired.) Drain peas and carrots. Put mixture in a serving bowl, add onions or shallots, butter, garlic powder, and salt and pepper. Mix well and serve hot.

4 to 6 servings

Bedford Falls Holiday Broccoli Casserole

2 (16-ounce) packages frozen broccoli
½ (9-ounce) package frozen corn
1 (24-ounce) carton cottage cheese
3 eggs
⅓ cup butter or margarine
⅓ cup all-purpose flour
2 cups shredded Swiss cheese
½ cup finely chopped onion
Salt and pepper to taste
8 slices bacon, cooked crisp and crumbled
10 whole wheat crackers, crushed

Preheat oven to 350 degrees F. Cook broccoli and corn, separately, according to package directions; drain. Combine cottage cheese, eggs, butter, and flour in a blender container; blend until smooth and set aside. Combine broccoli, corn, cheese, onion, and salt and pepper in a large mixing bowl; blend in cottage cheese mixture. Gently spoon into a greased 8×12×2-inch baking dish; sprinkle bacon and crushed crackers on top. Bake in preheated oven for 45 minutes.

8 to 10 servings

Q: What was the weather like on George and Mary's wedding day?

"Peter Bailey Picked a Peck of Peppers" Platter

This mixture is great served as a side dish, on sandwiches, or with freshly baked bread. The peppers can also be prepared outdoors on a barbecue.

2 large green bell peppers
2 large red sweet bell peppers
2 large yellow bell peppers
2 garlic cloves, chopped
5 tablespoons olive oil
1 small onion, chopped fine
4 tablespoons balsamic red wine vinegar
Salt and pepper to taste
¼ teaspoon oregano
3 tablespoons chopped parsley

Preheat broiler. Wash all peppers and place in a broiling pan 6 inches beneath heat. Watch peppers closely, as they will char quickly. As each side begins to blacken, rotate until as much skin as possible is blackened. Remove from broiler and wrap in wet towels or paper towels until cool. Peel off most of charred skin. Remove stems and seeds, and slice into strips. Put peppers in a large mixing bowl. Mix all other ingredients and pour over peppers, mixing until well covered.

6 to 8 servings

Frank's Creamed Capra Corn

18 ears fresh corn, shucked
½ cup water
3 tablespoons butter or margarine
Salt and pepper to taste

***A:** It was raining heavily.*

Place one end of each corn cob in the bottom of a large bowl. Using a sharp knife, cut the corn off the cob, but don't cut too deeply, as just the tops of the kernels are best. Use the blunt end of the knife to scrape the cob. This produces a lot of juice. Combine corn, juice, water, butter, and salt and pepper in a large saucepan. Simmer, uncovered, over low heat for about 10 to 15 minutes, stirring frequently to prevent burning. May be stored in freezer in sealed bags.

14 to 16 servings

Spinach Casserole

This is another great recipe from Carol Coombs Mueller, who played Janie Bailey in the film. Carol says this one will stick to your ribs!

2 (8-ounce) packages frozen chopped spinach
1 (10¾-ounce) can condensed cream of mushroom soup
1 cup shredded sharp Cheddar cheese
1 cup mayonnaise
1 small onion, chopped fine
1 egg, lightly beaten
1 cup whole wheat crackers, crushed
½ cup butter or margarine, melted

Preheat oven to 350 degrees F. In a medium saucepan, cook spinach according to package directions; drain. In a large mixing bowl, combine soup, cheese, mayonnaise, onion, and egg. Add spinach and mix well. Pour into 9×13×2-inch baking pan. Sprinkle crushed crackers over mixture and top with melted butter. Bake in preheated oven for 45 minutes.

8 to 10 servings

Q: Who caught the wedding bouquet?

Not a Smidge of Temperature Tomato and Onion Hodgepodge

4–5 large tomatoes, peeled and sliced
1 large onion, sliced
2 cucumbers, peeled and sliced
½ cup vegetable oil
2 tablespoons lemon juice
½ teaspoon dried oregano
Salt and pepper to taste
1 pinch of garlic powder
1 tablespoon chopped parsley

In a medium serving dish, alternate rows of tomato, onion, and cucumber slices. In a mixing bowl, combine all other ingredients well and pour over slices. Cover and refrigerate for 2 to 3 hours before serving.

8 to 10 servings

***A:** Violet Bick caught the bouquet.*

Desserts

"It's funny how powerful the sense of smell is and how many memories it can trigger. One of the things I remember most from my younger years is the smell of the movie sets. They smelled like cookies—that's the only way I can describe it. As I got older, that smell seemed to slowly disappear, and I remember how sad that was. I wish I could experience that smell again."

—*Jimmy Hawkins* (Tommy Bailey)

Cast picture

Quick 'n' Easy Carrot Spice Cake

This recipe was given by Todd Karns, who played Harry Bailey in the film. Todd is an artist and lives with his wife, Kate, in Mexico.

1¼ cups all-purpose flour
1⅛ cups packed dark brown sugar
1 teaspoon baking soda
1 teaspoon baking powder
2½ teaspoons cinnamon
½ teaspoon ground allspice
½ teaspoon salt
1⅓ cups shredded carrot
⅔ cup vegetable oil
2 eggs
1 (8-ounce) can crushed pineapple, well drained
1½ teaspoons vanilla
½ cup chopped walnuts

In a large mixing bowl, combine flour, brown sugar, baking soda, baking powder, cinnamon, allspice, salt, and carrots; mix well. Stir in oil, eggs, pineapple, and vanilla. Beat 2 minutes with a mixer, at medium speed. Stir in walnuts. Pour batter into a greased, 3-quart microwaveable dish with a cone. Cover with wax paper and cook at medium power for 11 minutes. A toothpick should come out clean when inserted in the center. Let stand for 10 to 15 minutes more. Cover and serve when ready.

8 to 10 servings

Q: How much money did the Baileys have for their honeymoon?

Janie's Fresh-Picked Strawberry Shortcake

2 cups all-purpose flour
2 teaspoons baking powder
1 teaspoon salt
2 tablespoons sugar
4 tablespoons softened butter or margarine
2/3 cup light cream
1/4 cup butter or margarine at room temperature
2 quarts strawberries, cleaned, topped, and sliced
1/2 cup sugar
Whipped cream

Preheat oven to 450 degrees F. In a large mixing bowl, combine flour, baking powder, salt, and sugar; sift well. Cut in butter with pastry blender until crumbly. Add light cream and mix well. On a lightly floured board, divide dough into two equal parts and roll out to 3/4 inch thickness. Place one half in a lightly-greased 9-inch cake pan. Spread butter on top. Place the second half on top of the buttered half. Bake in preheated oven for 10 to 12 minutes. Remove from oven and let cool for 5–10 minutes on a rack and split the halves. In a large serving dish, place one half of the shortcake. Place half of the strawberries on top. Sprinkle liberally with sugar. Put the other cake on top of the first and top with remaining strawberries. Serve with heaping dollops of whipped cream.

6 to 8 servings

***A:** They had $2,000.*

Richest Man in Town Chocolate Sheet Cake

BATTER

2 cups sugar
2 cups sifted all-purpose flour
1 teaspoon baking soda
½ teaspoon salt
1 cup (2 sticks) butter or margarine
5½ tablespoons cocoa
1 cup water
½ cup milk
2 eggs, well beaten
1¼ teaspoon vanilla

Preheat oven to 350 degrees F. In a large mixing bowl, sift sugar, flour, soda, and salt. In a small saucepan, over medium heat, melt butter. Add cocoa and water. Bring to a quick boil and pour over dry ingredients; mix well with mixer. Add milk, eggs, and vanilla, mix until blended. Pour batter in a greased 8×12×2-inch cake pan. Bake in preheated oven for 18 minutes, or until toothpick inserted in the center comes out clean.

FROSTING

1 stick butter or margarine
5½ tablespoons cocoa
6 tablespoons milk
1 pound confectioner's sugar
1 teaspoon vanilla

Place confectioner's sugar in a large mixing bowl. In a small saucepan, over medium heat, melt butter. Add cocoa and milk; stir. Bring to a quick boil. Slowly pour hot mixture over powdered sugar. Add vanilla, stir. Swirl over cake while still warm.

10 to 12 servings

Q: Where were they going on their honeymoon, and why didn't they go?

Snowy Night in Bedford Falls Ice Cake

1 (6-ounce) package semisweet chocolate chips
2 tablespoons water
1 tablespoon sugar
4 egg yolks, well beaten
4 egg whites, beaten
1 cup heavy cream, whipped
1 large store-bought angel food cake

In a double boiler, over low heat, place chocolate chips, water, sugar, and egg yolks; heat, stirring, until chips are melted. Let cool for a short while. Fold in egg whites. Fold in whipped cream. Break angel food cake into bite-size pieces. In a lightly buttered 8×8×2-inch cake pan, place half of the cake, then top with half the mix. Repeat this process. Cover and chill for 24 hours.

8 to 10 servings

Mr. Reinmann's German Chocolate Cake

BATTER

1 (4-ounce) bar sweet cooking chocolate
½ cup boiling water
2 cups sugar
1 cup (2 sticks) butter or margarine
4 egg yolks
1¼ teaspoons vanilla
2½ cups cake flour
1 teaspoon baking soda
1 teaspoon salt
1 cup milk
4 egg whites, well beaten

Preheat oven to 350 degrees F. In a small mixing bowl, dissolve chocolate bar in boiling water; let cool. In a large mixing bowl, mix sugar and butter with mixer until fluffy. Beat in egg yolks, one at a time, on low speed. Beat in dissolved chocolate and vanilla on low speed. Mix in flour, baking soda, salt, and milk, one

---

***A:** To New York for a week and to Bermuda for a week, but they were foiled by a bank run on the day they were to leave.*

item at a time, until batter is smooth. Pour batter in two well-greased 9×9×2-inch baking pans. Bake in preheated oven for approximately 40 to 45 minutes. Remove from oven and let cool for about 40 minutes in the pan. Place one layer on a serving plate. Put a layer of frosting, then add top layer. Frost top and serve.

FROSTING

1 cup sugar
1 cup sweetened condensed milk
(1 stick) butter or margarine
3 egg yolks
1¼ teaspoons vanilla
1¼ cups flaked coconut
1 cup pecans, chopped fine

In a medium saucepan, over medium heat, cook sugar, milk, butter, egg yolks, and vanilla, until thick, stirring occasionally. Stir in coconut and pecans. Beat with spoon until thick enough for frosting.

10 to 12 servings

Nick the Bartender's Rum Cake

1 (18-ounce) yellow cake mix
1 (4-ounce) package vanilla instant pudding mix
4 eggs
¾ cup dark rum
¼ cup water
½ cup oil
½ cup walnuts, crushed
Whipped cream

Preheat oven to 350 degrees F. In a large mixing bowl, combine cake mix, pudding mix, eggs, rum, water, and oil. Beat together with mixer on high speed for 2 minutes. Pour batter into a well-greased, floured tube pan. Sprinkle walnuts on top. Bake in preheated oven for 30 to 35 minutes or until toothpick inserted in center comes out clean. Let cake cool on wire rack for 15 minutes. Serve with a dollop of whipped cream.

10 to 12 servings

Q: What was the name of the old house?

Annie's Almond Tea Cakes

2 cups sugar
1 cup (2 sticks) butter or margarine
1 teaspoon lemon rind, grated
1 teaspoon orange rind, grated
3 egg whites
3½ cups all-purpose flour
1 teaspoon salt
1 teaspoon baking powder
¾ cup crushed almonds
3 tablespoons cinnamon

Preheat oven to 350 degrees F. In a large mixing bowl, cream butter and sugar together with mixer at low speed, for about 2 minutes. Add rinds and egg whites; mix well. In a separate bowl, sift together flour, salt, and baking powder. Blend with butter mixture for about a minute and chill uncovered for an hour. Roll to ¼ inch thickness on a lightly floured pastry sheet. Sprinkle almonds on top and cut into small squares. Place on a very lightly greased cookie sheet and sprinkle with cinnamon. Bake in preheated oven for 8 to 10 minutes or until golden brown.

5 to 6 dozen cookies

Angel Second Class Pink Lemon Pie

1 (12-ounce) can frozen pink lemonade
1 (14-ounce) can sweetened condensed milk
1½ cups of heavy cream, whipped
Red food coloring (optional)
1 graham cracker pie crust

In a blender container, mix pink lemonade and condensed milk and blend on low speed until thick, about 1 minute. Pour into a large mixing bowl and fold in whipped cream. If needed, mix in a drop or two of red food coloring until mixture turns desired shade of pink. Pour into graham cracker crust and refrigerate overnight.

6 to 8 servings

***A:** The old Granville house.*

Bert and Ernie's Coffee Break Coffee Cake

FILLING

½ cup dark brown sugar
1 cup walnuts, chopped
2 tablespoons cinnamon

In a medium bowl, mix togther the filling ingedients.

CAKE

1 cup (2 sticks) butter or margarine
2 cups sugar
6 eggs
1 teaspoon vanilla
1 pint sour cream
4 cups flour
½ teaspoon salt
1½ teaspoons baking powder
1 teaspoon baking soda

Preheat oven to 350 degrees F. In a large mixing bowl, mix butter, sugar, eggs, vanilla, and sour cream with mixer on low speed. In a separate bowl, sift together flour, salt, baking powder, and baking soda. Add to first mixture; beat well at medium speed for 1 minute. Pour ⅓ batter into an ungreased angel food pan. Sprinkle with ⅓ filling mixture. Alternate layers, with the filling ending up on top. Bake in a preheated oven for 1¼ to 1½ hours, or until a toothpick inserted in center comes out clean.

8 to 10 servings

Q: What was the address of the old house?

Mary's Homesick Applesauce Spice Cake

BATTER

1 cup (2 sticks) butter or margarine, room temperature
2 cups sugar
2 cups regular applesauce
3 cups all-purpose flour
1½ teaspoons cinnamon
½ teaspoon ground nutmeg
½ teaspoon ground mace
2 level teaspoons baking soda
1 teaspoon vanilla
1 cup pecans, chopped
1 cup raisins

Preheat oven to 350 degrees F. In a large mixing bowl, cream sugar and butter with mixer on low speed until fluffy, about 2 minutes. Fold in applesauce. In another large bowl, sift together flour, spices, and baking soda. Fold into butter mixture. Add vanilla, pecans, and raisins; mix well. Grease a 9-inch tube pan. Cut a circle of waxed paper to fit the bottom of the pan, and grease the paper. Pour batter in pan. Bake in preheated oven for 1½ hours, or until a toothpick inserted in center comes out clean. Remove from oven and let cool for 10 minutes. Turn cake out onto wire rack.

FROSTING

2 packed cups dark brown sugar
6 tablespoons heavy cream
¼ cup (½ stick) butter
½ teaspoon almond extract
1 cup confectioners' sugar

In a saucepan, over medium heat, combine brown sugar, cream, and butter. Bring to a slow boil, stirring occasionally. Remove from heat and stir in almond extract and sugar. Quickly pour over cooled cake, allowing frosting to roll down the sides.

10 to 12 servings

***A:** 320 Sycamore.*

Heaven Scent Cherry Cream Cheesecake

1¼ cup honey graham crackers, crushed
6 tablespoons butter or margarine, room temperature
11 ounces of cream cheese, softened
2 eggs, well beaten
¼ cup sugar
½ teaspoon vanilla
1 (16-ounce) can cherry pie filling
Whipped cream

Preheat oven to 350 degrees F. In a mixing bowl combine graham crackers and butter until well mixed. Press into bottom and sides of standard pie pan. In a large mixing bowl, blend cream cheese, eggs, sugar, and vanilla. Pour over graham cracker base. Bake in preheated oven for 20 minutes. Remove from oven and let cool in pan for 1 hour. Pour pie filling on top of cream cheese. Serve with dollop of whipped cream.

6 to 8 servings

Silent Snowfall Pound Cake

1 cup (2 sticks) butter, at room temperature
1 cup sugar
5 eggs
1 teaspoon almond extract
½ teaspoon vanilla extract
2 cups sifted all-purpose flour
Confectioners' sugar

Preheat oven to 350 degrees F. In a large mixing bowl, cream butter and sugar with mixer on low speed until fluffy, about 2 minutes. Gradually work in each egg, and beat well at medium speed after each addition. Add flavorings and gradually work in the flour, beating well at medium speed. Pour batter in a greased 9×5×3-inch bread pan. Bake in preheated oven for approximately 45 minutes, until a toothpick inserted in the center comes out clean.

8 to 10 servings

Q: Mary and George moved into the old house, and Mary spent numerous hours fixing it up while George went to the office. What was still not fixed, even at the end of the movie?

Bailey Kids' Strawberry Pretzel Delight

2 cups crushed pretzels
3/4 cup butter or margarine
3 tablespoons sugar
1 cup heavy cream
1 egg, lightly beaten
1 (8-ounce) package cream cheese, softened
1 cup confectioners' sugar
1 (6-ounce) package strawberry-flavored gelatin
2 cups boiling water
1 (12-ounce) package frozen strawberries, thawed

Preheat oven to 350 degrees F. In a large mixing bowl, mix pretzels, butter, and sugar. Press into 9×13×2-inch baking dish. Bake in preheated oven for 12 minutes. Let cool. In a large mixing bowl, combine heavy cream, egg, cream cheese, and confectioners' sugar, with a mixer; 30 seconds on low, then 1 minute on medium speed. Pour into crust. In a mixing bowl, dissolve gelatin in water and add thawed strawberries. Let cool in freezer for 5 minutes to thicken. Pour over top of crust and refrigerate until set.

8 to 10 servings

Bailey Holiday Maple Cake

1 1/4 cups maple sugar
1/2 cup (1 stick) butter or margarine, at room temperature
2 eggs, beaten
2 1/2 cups flour
1/2 teaspoon salt
1 teaspoon baking soda
1 teaspoon cinnamon
1/2 teaspoon ground nutmeg
1 1/2 cups regular applesauce
1 cup walnuts, chopped

***A:** The wooden ball on top of the newel post at the bottom of the stairs.*

Preheat oven to 350 degrees F. In a large mixing bowl, cream butter and maple sugar with mixer at low speed until fluffy, about 2 minutes. Add beaten eggs and blend thoroughly. In a separate bowl, sift together flour, salt, soda, and spices. Gradually add flour mixture and applesauce to butter mixture, alternating between the two; beat well. Fold walnuts into batter. Pour batter into a lightly greased 9×5×3-inch bread pan and bake in preheated oven for about 1 hour, or until a toothpick inserted in center comes out clean.

8 servings

Zuzu's Strawberry Rose Petal Pie

1 cup sugar
3 egg whites, beaten
16 Ritz crackers, crushed
½ teaspoon baking powder
⅔ cup pecans, crushed
1 pint fresh strawberries, washed and topped
1½ cups heavy cream, whipped
2 tablespoons confectioners' sugar, optional

Preheat oven to 350 degrees F. In a large mixing bowl, gradually add sugar to beaten egg whites; beat with wire wisk until stiff. In a separate bowl, combine crushed crackers and baking powder; add to egg whites. Add in pecans, mix until thick. Spread mixture over a greased 9-inch pie plate, pressing into place. Bake in preheated oven for 35 minutes. Let cool for an hour. Slice all but four strawberries. In a large mixing bowl, combine whipped cream and sliced strawberries. Place mixture in crust. Slice remaining strawberries and gently arrange into rose shapes on top of whipped cream. Sprinkle top with a fine layer of powdered sugar if desired. Refrigerate immediately. Chill for at least an hour before serving.

6 to 8 servings

Q: How many kids did the Baileys have?

Crabby Mother-in-Law Fruity Salad Cake

BATTER

1½ cups sugar
2 cups all-purpose flour
1 teaspoon baking soda
½ teaspoon salt
1 (3-ounce) can of fruit cocktail, with juice
2 eggs
1 teaspoon vanilla extract
½ cup dark brown sugar
½ cup walnuts, chopped

Preheat oven to 350 degrees F. In a large mixing bowl, sift together sugar, flour, baking soda, and salt. Add fruit cocktail with juice, and beat well with mixer on low to medium speed. Add eggs and vanilla, and beat for 1 minute on low to medium speed. Pour batter into a greased 9×13×2-inch baking pan. Sprinkle top with brown sugar and walnuts. Bake in preheated oven for 35 to 40 minutes, or until toothpick inserted in center comes out clean.

FROSTING

½ cup (1 stick) butter or margarine
½ cup sweetened condensed milk
¾ cup sugar
1 teaspoon vanilla extract
1 cup shredded coconut

In a saucepan, over low to medium heat, combine all ingredients except coconut. Heat to a slow boil for 2 minutes, stirring constantly. Remove from heat and add coconut. Drizzle over hot cake. Let cool and serve.

12 servings

***A:** George and Mary had four kids, Peter, Janie, Zuzu, and Tommy.*

Every Time a Bell Rings Rose Petal Pie

This is a variation of the recipe on page 155, using rose water. Rose water is available at fine food shops throughout the United States.

1 (10-ounce) package frozen sliced strawberries, thawed with juice
5½ tablespoons cornstarch
¾ cup sugar
½ teaspoon salt
3 cups milk
3 egg yolks
1½ tablespoons butter or margarine
½ teaspoon rose water
1 9-inch ready-made graham cracker pie crust
Whipped cream

Let strawberries thaw completely before cooking. In a medium saucepan combine strawberries with juice and 1 tablespoon of the cornstarch. Bring to a slow boil over medium heat, stirring constantly. Remove from heat and let stand. In a large mixing bowl, sift together remaining cornstarch with sugar and salt. Gradually add milk; stir until very smooth. Pour mixture into a medium saucepan and bring to a slow boil, over low to medium heat, stirring constantly; boil for 1 minute. Remove from heat, let cool slightly and carefully but quickly stir in egg yolks; mix well. Return to heat and bring to a boil for 1 minute, stirring constantly. Remove from heat and stir in butter and rose water. Let cool for 10 minutes. Spoon alternate layers of custard and strawberries into pie crust and swirl slightly with knife. Use some sliced strawberries to form roselike shapes on top. Refrigerate for at least 4 hours. Serve with dollops of whipped cream.

6 to 8 servings

Q: What Christmas carol was one of them playing over and over when George came home after Uncle Billy lost the money?

Ma Bailey's Prom Night Pumpkin Pie

2 eggs, lightly beaten
1 (16-ounce) can pumpkin
½ cup sugar
¼ cup dark brown sugar
½ teaspoon salt
1 teaspoon ground cinnamon
½ teaspoon ground ginger
¼ teaspoon ground cloves
½ teaspoon ground nutmeg
1⅔ cups sweetened condensed milk
Whipped cream
1 ready-made 9-inch pie crust (not graham cracker)

Preheat oven to 425 degrees F. Put all ingredients in a large mixing bowl and beat with mixer until well mixed, about 2 minutes on medium speed. Pour mixture into piecrust. Bake in preheated oven for 15 minutes. Reduce heat to 350 degrees F. and bake for an additional 40 minutes, or until knife inserted in center comes out clean. Let cool. Serve with generous dollops of whipped cream.

6 to 8 servings

"Zuzu, My Little Ginger Snap" Cookies

You didn't think for a second that I would leave out ginger snaps, did you? Here are several recipes that play on the ginger theme. Enjoy!

⅔ cup vegetable oil
1 cup sugar
1 egg
¼ cup molasses
2 cups all-purpose flour, well sifted
2 teaspoons baking soda
½ teaspoon salt
1½ teaspoons cinnamon
1 teaspoon ground ginger
½ teaspoon ground allspice
1 cup confectioners' sugar or brown sugar

A: *"Hark, the Herald Angels Sing."*

Preheat oven to 350 degrees F. In a large mixing bowl, mix oil and sugar, with mixer at low speed for 30 seconds. Add egg and mix well. Stir in molasses and mix well. In a separate bowl, sift together all other ingredients except confectioners' sugar. Add to mixture. Form into 1-inch balls and roll in powdered or brown sugar. Place 1 inch apart on a lightly greased cookie sheet and bake in preheated oven for 10 to 15 minutes, or until a toothpick inserted in the middle comes out clean.

About 3 to 4 dozen

Gingerbread

Another Zuzu favorite! Especially delicious when served warm with butter, honey, or a dollop of whipped cream.

½ cup (1 stick) butter or margarine, room temperature
½ cup dark brown sugar
¼ cup sugar
1 egg, beaten
2½ cups all-purpose flour
½ teaspoon baking soda
½ teaspoon salt
1 teaspoon ground cinnamon
1 teaspoon ground ginger
1 teaspoon ground cloves
1 cup molasses
1 cup hot water
Whipped cream (optional)

Preheat oven to 350 degrees F. In a large mixing bowl, combine butter, sugars, and beaten egg; beat until creamy, with mixer at low speed, about 1 minute. In a separate bowl, sift together flour, baking soda, salt, and spices. In a small bowl, dilute molasses in hot water. Gradually mix in molasses and dry ingredients into the creamed mixture, alternating between the two. Pour the batter into a lightly greased and floured 9×13-inch baking dish. Bake in preheated oven for about 45 minutes, or until toothpick inserted in center comes out clean.

12 servings

Q: What was the first word one of the kids asked George to spell?

Mary's Rainy Day Gingerbread People

This is a great rainy day project for mothers and kids. Dads, too! Have fun creating your own Bedford Falls characters!

1 cup molasses
4 tablespoons butter or margarine
1¼ teaspoons ground ginger
1 teaspoon baking soda
¼ teaspoon salt
½ teaspoon baking powder
2¼ cups all-purpose flour
Tube of icing, your choice of size and color
Various cake decorating doodads

In a small saucepan, over low to medium heat, bring molasses to a boil and add butter, stirring constantly. Remove from heat and pour into large mixing bowl. In a separate bowl, sift together all dry ingredients and add to molasses; mix well, with wooden spoon. Refrigerate for about an hour. Preheat oven to 400 degrees F. Roll mixture very thin on a floured pastry sheet and cut out people shapes with a cutter. Place shapes 1 inch apart on a lightly greased cookie sheet. Bake in preheated oven, about 4 to 6 minutes, checking to see they don't burn. Remove from cookie sheet with a spatula and let cool on 2 racks. *Decorate however you like!*

About 2 to 3 dozen, depending on size

Ma Bailey's Million-Dollar Brownies

2 1-ounce squares unsweetened chocolate
⅓ cup vegetable shortening
1 cup sugar
2 eggs, lightly beaten
1 teaspoon vanilla extract
¾ cup self-rising flour
¾ cup walnuts, chopped

A: *Peter asked him to spell "frankincense."*

Preheat oven to 350 degrees F. In a medium saucepan, heat chocolate and shortening over low heat until chocolate is completely melted, stirring constantly. Remove from heat. Stir in sugar, eggs, and vanilla; mix well. Add remaining ingredients; mix well. Pour into a greased 8×8×2-inch baking pan. Bake in preheated oven for about 30 to 35 minutes, or until toothpick inserted in center comes out clean. Let cool and cut into squares.

8 servings

Silver Bells Holiday Shapes Sugar Cookies

This is another fun project for the whole family!

1 cup (2 sticks) butter or margarine, at room temperature
1⅓ cups confectioners' sugar
1 egg
1 teaspoon vanilla extract
1 teaspoon almond extract
2½ cups self-rising flour
Sugar and dark brown sugar, as desired
Decorating doodads, as desired

In a large mixing bowl, combine butter, confectioners' sugar, egg, vanilla extract, and almond extract, with mixer on low speed for 1 minute. Gradually mix in flour. Cover and refrigerate for 2½ hours. Preheat oven to 375 degrees F. Scoop ¼ of the dough and roll to ¼-inch thickness on a lightly floured, cloth-covered pastry sheet. Cut into shapes. Repeat until all dough is used—as cookie sheets become available. Place shapes an inch apart on a lightly greased cookie sheet and sprinkle with regular or brown sugar. Bake in preheated oven for 7 minutes, or until edges turn light brown. Let cool for 3 to 5 minutes before removing from cookie sheet. Decorate to your heart's delight!

About 3 to 4 dozen, depending on size

Q: How many petals fell off a rose belonging to one of George's daughters—and which daughter?

Caribbean Coco-Berry-Chocolate Torte

3/4 cup flaked coconut
1 cup cake flour, sifted
1 teaspoon baking powder
1/4 teaspoon salt
4 eggs, separated
1 cup sugar
1 1/4 teaspoons vanilla extract
4 tablespoons butter or margarine, at room temperature
1/3 cup strawberry jam
2 (8 1/2-ounce) containers premade chocolate pudding
2–3 tablespoons confectioners' sugar
Whipped cream (optional)

Preheat oven to 350 degrees F. In a large mixing bowl, sift together 1/2 cup of the coconut, the flour, baking powder, and salt. In a separate bowl, beat egg whites until peaks form. Slowly beat in 1/2 cup sugar until whites are stiff. In a separate bowl, beat egg yolks, 1/2 cup sugar, vanilla, and butter until thick. Carefully fold egg yolk mixture into egg white mixture, then add flour mixture; blend slightly. Lightly grease an 8-inch springform pan, and coat bottom and sides with remaining coconut. Pour batter into pan and bake in preheated oven until top is brown, approximately 1 hour. Remove from oven and let cool completely in the pan, about an hour. Remove from pan and cut cake into three equal layers. Place one layer on a serving plate. Spread strawberry jam on top of layer. Add the second layer and, spread premade pudding on top. Add the final layer. Sprinkle confectioners' sugar on top. Even more delicious with a dollop of whipped cream.

8 servings

***A:** Three petals fell off Zuzu's rose.*

292-Year-Old English Toffee

1 cup sugar
1 cup (2 sticks) butter, room temperature
1 teaspoon vanilla extract
1 (12-ounce) package semisweet chocolate chips
½ cup chopped nuts, your choice

In a saucepan, combine sugar, butter, and vanilla. Bring to a boil over medium heat, stirring constantly. Spread a large piece of aluminum foil on table or board. Pour hot mixture over aluminum foil; let cool. In a double boiler, over medium to high heat, melt half of the chocolate chips; cool. Pour chocolate over one side of candy sheet, and sprinkle with half the chopped nuts, pressing them into place. Let stand until dry, about 30 minutes. Turn candy sheet over and repeat the process. Break into bite size pieces. Best if stored in metal tin!

About 1 pound of toffee

"She's a Peach" Cobbler

Best if served warm with vanilla ice cream or a dollop of whipped cream!

½ cup (1 stick) butter
¾ cup self-rising flour
1¼ cups sugar
½ cup milk
1 egg, beaten
2½ cups fresh peaches, sliced or diced
¼ cup honey graham crackers, crumbled

Preheat oven to 450 degrees F. In a saucepan, over low heat, melt butter. Pour butter into a 1½-quart casserole dish. In a separate bowl, combine flour, sugar, milk, and egg; mix well, with mixer on low speed for about a minute. Pour mixture into casserole. Place peaches on top of batter, but do not mix. Sprinkle graham crackers on top. Bake, uncovered, in preheated oven for about 35 minutes.

6 servings

Q: Where did George Bailey get his new suitcase?

Short-of-Bread Cookies

1 cup (2 sticks) butter, at room temperature
3/4 cup sugar
1 egg yolk
2 1/4 cups all-purpose flour
1/2 teaspoon salt

Preheat oven to 300 degrees F. In a large mixing bowl, cream butter and sugar until fluffy, with mixer on low speed, about 2 minutes. Beat in egg yolk. Add flour and salt and stir until well blended. Turn mixture out onto a floured pastry sheet and knead until smooth. Press dough into a 6×11-inch baking dish, until 3/4 inch thick, and prick all over with toothpick or fork. Bake, uncovered, in preheated oven for about 1 hour, or until lightly brown. Cut into rectangles or strips.

About 18 pieces

Zuzu's After-School Cherry Delight

1 3/4 cups sugar
1 cup (2 sticks) butter, at room temperature
4 eggs
1 1/4 teaspoons vanilla extract
2 1/2 cups self-rising flour
1 (16-ounce) can cherry pie filling
Whipped cream (optional)

Preheat oven to 350 degrees F. In a large mixing bowl, combine sugar, butter, eggs, and vanilla and beat with a mixer for 2 minutes on low speed. Gradually mix in flour. Reserve 1 1/2 cups of batter. Pour remaining batter into a lightly greased jelly roll pan. Cover batter with cherry pie filling. Drop remaining batter over filling by spoonfuls. Bake in preheated oven for about 35 to 40 minutes, or until golden brown. Cut into squares and serve with a dollop of whipped cream, if desired.

8 to 10 servings

***A:** World Luggage and Sporting Goods Store, 417 Genesee Street.*

Zuzu Clusters

12 ounces semisweet chocolate chips
12 ounces peanut butter chips
1 (12-ounce) jar salted peanuts
2 tablespoons milk

In a double boiler, over medium heat, heat chocolate chips until melted; set aside. In a medium saucepan, heat peanut butter chips and milk until melted. Add melted chocolate and peanuts; stir. Drop by spoonfuls on waxed paper or cookie sheet. Refrigerate for 2 to 3 hours. Best if stored covered in refrigerator.

Makes 2 to 3 dozen pieces

Karolyn's Krispy Kringles

1/3 cup butter or margarine
2/3 cup semisweet chocolate chips
1/2 cup sugar
1 egg, beaten
1/2 cup all-purpose flour, sifted
Pinch salt
1 1/4 teaspoons vanilla extract
1/2 cup walnuts, chopped

Preheat oven to 400 degrees F. In a double boiler, over medium heat, heat butter and chocolate chips until completely melted, stirring constantly. Remove from heat and add sugar. When sugar is dissolved, beat well. Add egg, flour, salt, and vanilla; mix well. Pour into greased 11×15×1-inch baking pan. Sprinkle with nuts. Bake in preheated oven for 12 minutes. Let cool. Cut into squares.

Makes about 3 dozen

Q: What movie was playing at the Bijou when George was running through the street at film's end?

Holiday Raspberry-Chocolate Bars

This is a very special recipe given to me by Virginia Patton-Moss, who played Ruth Dakin-Bailey in the film. She got the recipe from Beulah Bondi, who played the senior Mrs. Bailey.

2½ cups all-purpose flour
1 cup sugar
¾ cup pecans, chopped fine
2 sticks (1 cup) butter, at room temperature
1 egg
1 (12-ounce) jar seedless red raspberry jam
1⅔ cups semisweet chocolate chips

Preheat oven to 350 degrees F. In a large bowl, combine flour, sugar, pecans, butter, and egg; stir until crumbly. Set aside 1½ cups of the mixture. Press remaining mixture into the bottom of a lightly greased 9×13×2-inch baking pan. Spread the raspberry jam over top. Sprinkle with chocolate chips and remaining crumb mixture. Bake in preheated oven for 40 to 45 minutes, or until lightly brown. Cool completely in pan; cut into 2×2-inch bars.

24 bars

Chairman of the Eats Committee Cherry Pie

1½ cups sugar
⅓ cup all-purpose flour
2 (1-pound) cans pitted red tart cherries, drained
½ teaspoon almond extract
Butter as desired
1 premade 8-inch piecrust (not graham cracker)

Preheat oven to 425 degrees F. In a large mixing bowl, mix sugar and flour. Blend in cherries and almond extract. If not packaged in a pan, put piecrust in an 8 inch pie pan. Pour ingredients into piecrust; top with small dots of butter. Bake in preheated oven for 30 to 35 minutes, or until edges are light brown. *Optional:* Use

---

A: The Bells of St. Mary's, *with Bing Crosby.*

a second premade crust for the top of the pie. Place second crust on top, cut away excess, and pinch edges together. Cut slits in top. Increase baking time to about 40 minutes. Be careful that juices don't overflow too much! If pie looks done ahead of time, don't be afraid to take it out of the oven.

6 to 8 servings

Little George's World Explorer Coconut Macaroons

This recipe was given to me by Bobbie Anderson, who played young George Bailey in the film. When young Mary turned down George's offer for coconut on her ice cream from Gower's, he said, "Say, brainless, don't you know where coconuts come from?" Bobbie now lives with his wife in California.

½ cup egg whites
1 tablespoon cornstarch
1 tablespoon vanilla extract
1¼ cups sugar
¼ teaspoon salt
2¼ cups shredded coconut

Preheat oven to 350 degrees F. In a large mixing bowl, beat egg whites until stiff. Stir in sugar gradually. Place egg mixture into double boiler over simmering water. Heat until warm, but not hot, Add all remaining ingredients. Remove from heat and mix well. Drop by spoonful about an inch apart onto a cookie sheet lined with parchment paper. Bake in preheated oven for 20 minutes or until tops are lightly browned. Cool on racks.

2 dozen macaroons

Q: What was written on Mrs. Hatch's mailbox?

Clarence Oddbody's Heavenly Strawberry-Banana Dessert

This is a favorite of Carol Coombs's family. Carol played Janie Bailey in the movie. She is now a retired schoolteacher living in California.

CRUST

2 cups crushed unsalted pretzels
¾ cup melted butter or margarine
3 tablespoons sugar

FILLING

2 cups heavy cream
1 (8-ounce) package cream cheese, softened
1 cup sugar

TOPPING

1 (6-ounce) package strawberry gelatin
2 cups boiling water
1 large banana, sliced
2 (16-ounce) packages frozen strawberries with syrup, thawed

Preheat oven to 350 degrees F. In a medium mixing bowl, combine crust ingredients until crumbly and press into an ungreased 9×13×2-inch baking pan. Bake in preheated oven for 10 minutes; let cool. In a large mixing bowl, beat cream, cream cheese, and sugar with mixer on low speed until smooth, about 2 minutes. Spoon into cooled crust and spread top evenly. In a large bowl, dissolve gelatin in boiling water. Stir in strawberries with syrup and banana slices. Chill in refrigerator until partially set, about 15 minutes. Carefully spoon over filling. Chill 4 to 6 hours. Cut into squares and serve.

10 to 12 servings

***A:** The mailbox read "Mrs. J. W. Hatch."*

Christmas With Karolyn

"The thing I remember most about filming the movie is the Christmas tree in the Bailey house. It was the biggest Christmas tree I had ever seen. It was beautifully decorated with beaded ornaments that looked like they came from fairyland. I remember getting in trouble with my mom for touching the tree—I couldn't resist!"

—*K.G.*

The Bailey family at the Christmas tree.

Christmas has traditionally been the biggest and probably the most important meal at my house. It's a time for all the family to gather and discuss what the year has been like and what the future might hold. It's also a time to reflect for a moment on all blessings this life has to offer. Here are some of my favorite recipes for a bountiful Christmas Day feast. These should easily feed twelve to fifteen people. I hope you enjoy them!

Holiday Turkey

Do not stuff turkey until it's time to bake it!

1 22-pound turkey

If turkey is frozen, begin the thawing process two or three days in advance. Preheat oven to 325 degrees F. Wash turkey thoroughly, inside and out. Stuff with chestnut stuffing (recipe follows). Place turkey in a roasting pan breast side up. Make an aluminum foil tent over turkey. Roast in preheated oven for 7 to 7½ hours. Remove foil for the last 30 to 45 minutes. Remove turkey and place on large platter.

Q: What was the new home development by the Building & Loan called and what was Potter's called?

Chestnut Stuffing

1 (12-ounce) package herbed stuffing mix
1 (12-ounce) package cornbread stuffing mix
2 (6-ounce) cans sliced water chestnuts, drained
2 cups chopped celery
2 cups chopped onions
2 cups milk
1 cup turkey broth, if needed
Salt and pepper to taste
Pinch of garlic powder

In a large mixing bowl, combine all ingredients well, using a wooden spoon or your hands. Gently stuff dressing into turkey. Do not pack hard because dressing will expand. Combine any leftover dressing with enough turkey broth to moisten it and place in a casserole dish. Bake extra stuffing in preheated 350-degree oven for about an hour, until warmed through and slightly crisp on top.

12 to 15 servings

Turkey Gravy

Pan drippings from roasted turkey
1 cup water
1–2 tablespoons flour
3 (1.2-ounce) packages of prepared turkey gravy

After removing turkey from roasting pan, skim off as much fat as possible. Shake flour and water together in a closed container. Gradually add to pan drippings, stirring constantly. Prepare package gravy according to directions and add to homemade gravy. Heat and serve.

12 to 15 servings

***A:** Bailey Park and Potter's Field.*

Traditional Mashed Potatoes

16 medium white potatoes, peeled
1–2 cups milk
4 tablespoons butter or margarine
Salt and pepper to taste

Cut potatoes into chunks. In a soup pot, place potatoes and enough water to cover and boil until tender, about 20 minutes. Drain. Put potatoes back in pot; mash until almost smooth. Add milk, butter, salt and pepper and beat with mixer on medium speed until fluffy. Adjust seasoning until desired flavor results. (Tasting while cooking is one of the benefits of being the chef!)

12 to 15 servings

Karolyn's Favorite Sweet Potato Casserole

3 cups sweet potatoes, cooked, peeled, and mashed
1 cup sugar
1/2 cup (1 stick) butter or margarine
1 teaspoon lemon juice
2 eggs
1/2 teaspoon cinnamon
1 cup dark brown sugar
3/4 cup chopped pecans
1/3 cup flour
1/3 cup butter or margarine

Preheat oven to 350 degrees F. In a large mixing bowl, mix mashed sweet potatoes, sugar, butter, lemon juice, and eggs with wooden spoon. Pour mixture into a lightly greased 3-quart casserole. In a separate medium bowl, mix remaining ingredients together thoroughly and sprinkle on top of sweet potato mixture. Bake, uncovered, in preheated oven for 15 minutes, or until lightly browned.

12 to 15 servings

Q: What was the toast and gifts George and Mary give to the Martinis at their new home?

Green Beans and Bacon

4 (16-ounce) cans whole green beans, partially drained
1 small onion, chopped fine
8 slices bacon, cooked crisp and crumbled

In a medium saucepan, combine green beans, onions, and bacon. Simmer until hot, about 20 minutes, and serve.

12 to 15 servings

Frank's Creamed Capra Corn

see recipe on page 140

Broccoli Salad

1 (16-ounce) package broccoli florets
1 cup dry-roasted peanuts
1 cup raisins
1 pound sliced bacon, cooked crisp and crumbled
4 green onions with tops, chopped fine
1 cup mayonnaise
2 teaspoons sugar
1 teaspoon distilled white vinegar
Salt and pepper

In a large serving bowl, mix broccoli, peanuts, raisins, bacon, and onion. In a separate bowl, mix remaining ingredients. Pour dressing over salad and toss.

12 to 15 servings

***A:** "Bread, that this house will never know hunger; salt, that life may always have flavor; and wine, that joy and prosperity may reign forever."*

Cranberries

2 (16-ounce) cans jellied cranberries
2 (16-ounce) cans of prepared cranberries

Pour jellied cranberries onto serving dish and slice. Pour prepared cranberries into a bowl and serve. Garnish both with celery leaves.

12 to 15 servings

Sunday Come-to-Dinner Rolls

see recipe on page 69

Bailey Kids' Strawberry Pretzel Delight

see recipe on page 154

Ma Bailey's Prom Night Pumpkin Pie

see recipe on page 158

Egg Nog

see recipe on page 35

Movie Mishaps

Real hard-core It's a Wonderful Life *buffs have probably spotted some of the movie's mishaps—but maybe not. Some are obvious, others are tricky. See if you know these. . . .*

In one of the film's more memorable moments, George and Uncle Billy are exiting the Bailey house the day of Harry and Ruth's wedding party. Uncle Billy is smashed and can't find the hat on his head or his way home. George points him in the right direction and as Uncle Billy leaves a prop man accidentally knocks over a stack of empty film canisters, which sounds like Uncle Billy falling over some old garbage cans. George's reaction was perfect, and Capra let the scene run. Uncle Billy spontaneously called out, "I'm all right! I'm all right!" The prop man thought for sure he would be fired for messing up the scene. Instead, Capra used the cut as is and gave the man a $10 bonus!

In one of the more glaring mistakes, George Bailey is walking down Main Street on Christmas Eve, carrying a wreath and a stack of newspapers that tell about Harry's heroics in World War II. The wreath is on his arm as he walks down the street and into the Building & Loan. Harry is on the phone from Washington, and as George takes the phone to talk to him, he places the wreath on the desk. The next shot shows George talking to Harry with the wreath still on his arm! Apparently, Capra had cut the scene for some reason, and when shooting resumed, no one could remember where the wreath was supposed to be.

Everyone knows the words to "Auld Lang Syne," right? Don't tell that to Zuzu! At the end of the film, Zuzu is resting in George Bailey's arms near the Christmas tree. It's just been announced that Sam Wainwright will advance George up to $25,000, and everyone breaks into "Should old acquaintance be forgot . . ." If you watch closely, Zuzu is trying desperately to sing along, but nobody taught her the words before shooting began! You can almost see the frustration on her face.

If you look closely at the full cast picture on page 144, you'll see Zuzu to the right side of the picture. Two things are strange here. First, she appears to be pointing at something, and second, there is a big letter K on her coat. When asked about this, Karolyn Grimes didn't have the vaguest idea of what she was pointing at. As for the pin, K obviously stands for Karolyn. Her mom forgot to take it off before the shot was taken. The photographer never caught it!

Here's one from an insider: Jimmy Stewart had been away from movies during the war and he was nervous about his love scene with Donna Reed, fearing he had lost his "technique." He delayed as long as he could, find an alibi. Finally, Capra said it had to be now. Reluctantly, Stewart did the scene, now considered one of the hottest love scenes ever. Stewart and Reed were magic, and the scene was completed in one take. Capra was thrilled. However, the script girl approached Capra and agreed that it was good, but that they had dropped a whole page of dialogue. Capra retorted, "With technique like that, who needs dialogue!"

Happy George Bailey is surrounded by family after his visit with Clarence.

Suggested Menus

Thanksgiving Dinner With Karolyn

Holiday Turkey
Chestnut Stuffing
Turkey Gravy
Traditional Mashed Potatoes
Karolyn's Favorite Sweet Potato Casserole
Green Beans and Bacon
Creamed Corn
Broccoli Salad
Cranberries
Sunday Come-to-Dinner Rolls
Bailey Kids' Strawberry Pretzel Delight
Pumpkin Pie
Eggnog

Bailey Park Picnic

Saturday BBQ With the Baileys
Bedford Falls Famous Barbecued Country Ribs
Bailey Park Picnic Coleslaw
Ma Bailey's Summertime Vegetable Tray
Victory Garden Potato Salad
Annie's Old-fashioned Apple Pie
J. W. Hatch's Sourpuss Home-Style Lemonade
Violet Bick's Devilish Eggs

The Dakin-Bailey Wedding Reception Feast

Hammy Sammy Wainwright Roll-ups
Ruth Dakin's Bacon Wraps
Cousin Tillie's Saucy Meatballs
Billy Bailey's Irish Coffee
Ice Cream Social Almond Tea Cakes
Richest Man in Town Chocolate Sheet Cake
Cousin Tillie's Fruity-Fizz Punch

Zuzu's Fourth of July Birthday Bash (Karolyn's Birthday!)

Annie's Southern Fried Chicken
Karolyn's Cheesy Potatoes
Macaroni alla Martini
Bailey's Baked Beans and Bacon
Bedford Falls Corn Bake
Fresh Watermelon

South Seas Rainy-Day Luau

George's Lust for Adventure Mandarin Salad
"I Must Be Off My Nut" Banana Bread
South Pacific Honeymoon Chicken
George Bailey's "The One That Got Away" Tahitian Swordfish Steaks
Exotic Wedding Night Luau Roast
Violet Bick's Always Creamy Rice
Caribbean Coco-Berry-Chocolate Torte

Index of Recipes

Printed in the United States
65929LVS00009B/77

9 780806 521657